LUTHERAN

VOICES

Who Do You Say That I Am?
21st Century Preaching

Susan K. Hedahl

Foreword by Adele Stiles Resmer

Augsburg Fortress
Minneapolis

OTHER LUTHERAN VOICES TITLES

Large-quantity purchases or custom editions of these books are available at a discount from the publisher. For more information, contact the sales department at Augsburg Fortress, Publishers, 1-800-328-4648, or write to: Sales Director, Augsburg Fortress, Publishers, P.O. Box 1209, Minneapolis, MN 55440-1209.

See www.lutheranvoices.com

Dedicated to

The Women's Theological Class
St. James Lutheran Church
Gettysburg, Pennsylvania

Those living faithfully with the questions

WHO DO YOU SAY THAT I AM?
21st Century Preaching

Editor: Scott Tunseth

Cover Design: Koechel Peterson and Associates, Inc., Minneapolis, MN
          www.koechelpeterson.com

Cover photo: The Sanctury, St. Andrew's Lutheran Church, Mahtomedi, MN
          Koechel Peterson and Associates, Inc., Minneapolis, MN

ISBN 0-8066-4990-9

Manufactured in the U.S.A.

07   06   05   04   03   2   3   4   5   6   7   8   9   10

Contents

Foreword

What is Lutheran preaching, and why is it that—given the good, bad and the ugly of any particular sermon heard in recent memory—we continue to care about it? Because truth is, we do care and care deeply. We care about preaching because Scripture and the Lutheran tradition promises that we meet Jesus, crucified and raised, in the preached Word. We care because in that encounter with Jesus, our complicated and gifted lives are held in relationship with the living God, and we are individually and collectively renewed in a deep and meaningful way. We care because the Holy Spirit sparks our "caring," pulling us to the Word.

Given these realities, it is significant that Professor Hedahl begins and ends her discussion of Lutheran preaching with Jesus, the very one we seek. She deftly guides us through the tradition that places preached Word at its center and highlights significant benchmarks within the tradition. I expect you will be particularly drawn to her understanding of the tradition that "delights in the tensions and paradoxes that characterize human relationships with God," inviting us into discussions of justification and sanctification, law and gospel, faith and grace. She grounds Lutheran tradition deep in its Scriptural roots and brings it into conversation with 21st century realities that stretch and challenge it. Diverse cultural and ecumenical forms of preaching, using the language of science, medicine and psychology, and addressing seekers and life-long Christians are just a few of the realities Professor Hedahl notes. The particular gift of this book is the conversation between the rich Lutheran tradition and its understanding of preaching and the current world in which preaching is challenged to engage new and confounding realities.

As Professor Hedahl herself says, this book is not the final answer to "what is Lutheran preaching?" Rather it is a beginning point, a place to start but not end discussion that will go on long after you close the last page of this book. Her comments on the role of the sermon listener will likely generate lively conversation about the hearer of the Word and your role before, during, and after the preaching event. Likewise, I would imagine that many preachers, novice and experienced alike, will continue to wrestle with the relationship between Scripture, tradition, the sciences, and the world around us in an attempt to be faithful to the Word that we are called to preach. Together, we will want to examine further the relationship between preaching, worship, the sacraments, and the rich community with which it is in dialogue. Professor Hedahl invites us to look anew at Lutheran preaching and, in so doing, invites us on a journey toward the Jesus we seek and the very One who finds us.

ADELE STILES RESMER
THE LUTHERAN SEMINARY AT PHILADELPHIA

Preface

Preaching the good news of Jesus Christ has always been at the heart of our Lutheran Christian faith. Its proclamation tradition is rooted in the Bible and finds its later flowering in the writings of the Reformation era. Today the faith we proclaim continues to speak to us from the many dedicated preachers, both ordained and lay, who preach this gospel on a regular basis.

This book will examine what preaching looks like traditionally and what changes it is now encountering in the context of a rapidly changing, pluralistic world. It offers resources for both preachers and listeners so they may ponder and possibly enhance the preaching event in their particular faith community together.

Many people and resources are presented in this book. They represent the preachers, students, and colleagues who have always given me a great deal to think about over the years. It is to them that this book is dedicated!

The New Testament speaks occasionally of the "mysteries of our faith." As such, this book seeks to honor all the mysterious, unbelievable, and yet believable events related to the life, death, and resurrection of Jesus Christ and the privilege we have to speak and hear that good news week after week.

Introduction

Who Do You Say That I Am?

"They came to Philip, who was from Bethsaida in Galilee, and said to him, 'Sir, we wish to see Jesus.'"

⇸ *John 12:21*

Posing the question

"Who do you say that I am?" This was Jesus' question for his original band of followers and other interested onlookers. Saul fearfully asked his own form of that question. On the Damascene road when he heard a voice addressing him, he asked, "Who are you, Lord?" Mary, in tears in the garden after the Crucifixion, assumes Jesus is the gardener and asks him where Jesus' body is. This is *the* identity question most central to all the Gospels. Throughout the books of the New Testament, it is a question that is given various partial and multifaceted answers.

Jesus is by turns identified as Lord, Savior, Master, Friend, Rabbi, Son of Man, Son of Mary, Lamb of God, King of the Jews, the Christ, Son of God, Shepherd. The history of human faith has added its own terms: Friend of Sinners, Beautiful Savior, Lord of the Nations, Holy Child, Prince of Peace, Brother, Font of Grace, Living Word, Word of God, Bread of Life, and Redeemer.

Jesus' question prompts another question for both preachers and listeners: "How does his question *preach*?" At every Christian worship service that includes proclamation, in every time and place, Jesus' question and the manner it is proclaimed engage in dialogue with one another. The Christian preacher's work is *always* to respond in some measure to Jesus' question, whether this means speaking of his personality, words, activities, attributes, presence, or the realities of his divinity and his humanity. As a result, the preacher's verbal work becomes the work of the people. The sermon, or homily, urges them to answer the question for themselves as a corporate expression of the faithful and as individual practitioners of the Christian faith.

In whatever forms the gospel is proclaimed, Jesus' question radiates from their center. At its core it is an invitation to choose life at its fullest. His question runs parallel to those certitudes of our faith that we proclaim: God in Jesus Christ is at work among us through the work of the Holy Spirit. Jesus himself not only proclaimed his mission and nature but also effectively placed his assertions in tension with an all-pervasive question, "Who do you say that I am?" His question thus both challenges and nurtures our beliefs in his life and works.

In couching the question of his identity in personal language, Jesus' statement is also an invitation. It is a relational question, a "you" and "me" query that asks us to claim a different ground contrary to that of rote response. When confronted with Jesus' question, we do not stand on neutral ground. Instead, we meet Jesus and ponder his scrutiny of our presence before him!

There is a divine ruthlessness about Jesus' question that holds us accountable, for he is asking of us—everything. The author of a medieval preaching manual recognizes this insistent Godly attention in our lives. The image he suggests to the preachers of his day is a unique illustration, based on the nobleman's prized hunter and bird of prey, the falcon.

And above all else, do not desist from giving your heart to Christ. For he himself has said in Proverbs 23: "Son, lend me your heart." A noble bird of prey takes nothing else from its prey but its clean heart, and Christ does not deal otherwise with his prey that he has redeemed with his precious blood. Therefore, Augustine says, "From the Father's bosom he descended into the heart of the Virgin, like a noble bird that seeks nothing but the heart."[1]

The context of the question today

Jesus' question still stands. What nuances his question, however, is the context in which we consider it today. We can describe this context in a very general way as "postmodern." The term is laden with multiple meanings and used in areas of human thought that include literature, philosophy, sociology, and history. This term has been used to describe the radical changes in human life brought about by education, technology, an increased awareness of global pluralism, and emerging multiple definitions of the nature of truth.

The term "postmodern" not only attends to the outward changes in human life but also includes an effort to discern and define what impact these changes have on people's ways of thinking, believing, and living. Various authors would define these changes as

- creating a mood of uncertainty regarding life's purpose and meaning;
- a refusal to affiliate with any one point of view exclusively;
- a questioning of what constitutes power and authority and the nature of truth;
- creating a need to identify one's own position within a shifting environment of many lifestyles and options.

As a result, it is possible to view the "postmodern" context as either the grounds for despair or as a way of framing life's many options more enthusiastically.

Since the overall mood of the postmodern context is a questioning one, Jesus' question itself offers the best entry into this unfolding 21st century world of Lutheran proclamation. In this book the term "postmodern" is used to examine the contemporary context of preaching and its history, challenges, and new changes. It will look at how the characteristics of the postmodern era have influenced preaching. Through the method of postmodern questioning itself, it will invite the reader to identity where she or he is within that context through the template of Jesus' question.

Thus, throughout this work, I define "postmodern" in relationship to preaching as a *context* issue. It describes today's world in which people must confront and consider many different, sometimes conflicting, points of view about reality and truth. In this postmodern world people must decide within their own context which point(s) of view and truth claims will determine how they lead their lives. postmodern proclamation must take into consideration this multifaceted context by using Jesus' question as the foundation of all proclamation. For his question enables the postmodern preacher and listener to continue the rich dialogue between God and humanity about what constitutes salvation and life.

Models and means to preach Jesus' question today

Jesus' question appeals to the human need to understand life's tremendous complexities and crosscurrents. It engages the human listener in asking key questions about God, about relationships, and the meaning of life. It offers a way to begin thinking about how preaching can faithfully respond to these intersections of life and faith.

In each generation new models are developed that attempt to explain how the gospel stands in some type of relationship with the world. Resulting theological ideas and models have been instructive for the work of the preacher. Because of them, a number of preaching responses have emerged that specifically discuss how proclamation might sound in the postmodern context. Some of these faith life proposals were effective primarily for their own era, and some strands of various models have survived over time. New models of the relationship between gospel and context are always being proposed.[2]

These faith life models offer many perspectives, all of which significantly affect preaching choices. Proclamation can thus choose from such different approaches as:

Vantage points—Some of these pulpit perspectives preach a radical separation of the listener from the contemporary context, so as to affirm the gospel's claims in counter distinction from the world; some proclaim an intricate merger of gospel with cultural influences and themes; others preach a model that presents a set of faith/life tensions that the listener/believer can affirm.

Components of the preaching task—These models focus specifically on the different roles of the preacher, the congregation, the individual listener, or the contents of what is preached.

The means by which the gospel is proclaimed—This includes utilizing forms other than the traditional monologic sermon addressed to silent listeners. Such forms include drama, dialogue, and the use of technology ranging from a slide projector to Internet capabilities. All of these provide different ways to assist the preacher and listeners more actively participate in the act of proclamation. As one engages Jesus' question from a homiletical point of view, one must thus do so with these realities in mind:

- traditional and contemporary means of gospel proclamation;
- sociological and homiletical faith life models developed from various academic fields;
- ways in which the postmodern context affects both the preparation and witness of the preacher and the lives of the listeners and practioners of the Christian faith.

This book will view gospel proclamation through the lenses of Jesus' question with the understanding that it can highlight those historical gifts of Lutheran preaching and also rework these same gifts within the context of a postmodern world, whose views offer significant challenges to the content of our gospel and the means by which we proclaim it.

What's ahead?

Chapter One, "The Lutheran in Lutheran Preaching," will examine what is "Lutheran" about Lutheran preaching. Christian preaching generally is a happily notorious endeavor that is eclectic in style and far ranging in its theological foci. Much Christian preaching also tends to be intuitively, if not explicitly, ecumenical and inter-cultural because of the vast range of topics and biblical perspectives used. But what are the Lutheran sermonic watermarks—those theological and rhetorical goals and sources Lutherans commonly employ in preaching a Lutheran sermon? Luther and the Reformers closest to him in time never wrote a book or monograph on the topic "The Lutheran Sermon," but the basic Reformation documents definitely provide a framework for determining some answers to that question.

Finally, the chapter will look at today's Lutheran sermon and ask how the traditional, Reformation-derived principles for preaching are still present, absent, or newly reconfigured in today's gospel proclamation in a postmodern world.

Chapter Two, "It's the Gospel Truth: The Bible, Lectionary, and Preaching," will assess the centrality of the Bible in Lutheran preaching today. While most Lutherans assert its importance in an unqualified and genuine way, the question is more complex when other factors are taken into consideration. These include issues such as "preaching the Bible" as compared to "preaching the lectionary," the influence of other forms of communication and knowledge on the authority and truth claims of the Bible, and the changing understanding of the biblical mindsets in conversation with contemporary life.

Chapter Three, "The Life of a Lutheran Sermon," will explore how the preaching event is related to its classical rhetorical roots and a collection of other variables that profoundly and uniquely affect each sermon's construction. Readers will have an opportunity to see how sermonic variables are formed by context through the example of an ordination sermon.

One of the more formative parts of the Sunday preaching event is, believe it or not, the pulpit! Chapter Four, "The Pulpit: A Look at he Preaching Furniture," discusses how architecture can have both cultural and rhetorical effects on the listeners and shape the way they hear sermons. It will explore how the pulpit impacts on the way people both hear and respond to Jesus' identity question.

One of the major homiletics areas that has undergone a lot of scrutiny in the past decade is the role of *both* proclaimer and listeners. This is the topic of Chapter Five, "Who Is Preaching? Who Is Listening?" With contemporary desires to hear preaching as less of an authoritarian address and more mutual conversation, the chapter will look at the commonly understood functions of the preacher and the reasons for a renewed focus on the role of the listener in preaching (silence speaks volumes!). It will offer suggestions (by way of approval) for how this mutual way of sharing the gospel might enhance worship communities. The relationship of preacher and listeners is a fascinating one, since it contains a significant number of issues related to authority, the speech/silence continuum, interpretation, and ethical and spiritual formation.

Chapter Six, "Only Jesus: The Elusive and Intimate God," utilizes another biblical episode, the Transfiguration, to describe the struggles of contemporary preaching in sorting out the relationship between the Christ of faith and the Jesus of history. Theologically, this area of preaching is taking on heightened significance in the face of increasing global and communal pluralism. Just which Jesus do we proclaim when we preach? How is Jesus' own question heard in a pluralistic, postmodern context?

The chapter will assess a wide variety of interpretations of the historical Jesus ranging from ethnic to ideological views, including the more general cultural views that determine the type of jewelry sold, the songs sung, the mottos inscribed, and the sermon filler materials some preachers resort to. This overview will be compared to the general Lutheran views of the person of Jesus Christ proclaimed in most pulpits and then ask how these views of Jesus have been affected by the postmodern setting.

Chapter Seven, "Lutheran Voices: Witnesses to Life," will summarize those traditional features of Lutheran preaching. The chapter will pose questions regarding the contemporary purpose and meaning of today's Lutheran preaching. Further, the chapter's contents will identify some different ways of looking at the treasures of our preaching tradition and practices as a way of offering these gifts to our own communities and to ecumenical and interfaith communities.

"Appendix: Assessing the Sermon" will offer a congregation survey, a set of questions on texts, and two sermon assessment forms that listeners and preacher alike can use in discussing and analyzing the act of preaching and specific sermons.

By way of definition

Those who write about preaching use definitions that vary greatly from book to book, tradition to tradition, time to time. Where one author might describe the reality of sermonic "structure," another will use "homiletical moves" in its place. While one writer describes the use of images in preaching, another may speak in a slightly different way of the same thing and use the term "story." In this volume, I use the following definitions. Some of them are "Lutheran," while others belong more closely to the long tradition of preaching generally.

The word "preaching" in this work is used interchangeably with the word "proclamation," although this latter term is often meant to include sharing the gospel in other ways besides the pulpit. Further, "sermon" and "homily" are also used interchangeably and in a very general way, although their meanings are more complicated historically. Sermon is variously defined as something longer than a homily!

A particular type of preaching called "sermon" also was well developed by Luther's time. It relied heavily on forms of medieval philosophy and logic to get its points across. Luther considered such preaching often unintelligible and too abstract theologically for most listeners. As a result he both urged and developed a plainer style of preaching. Today most Lutheran listeners understand a sermon as anywhere from 10 to 20 minutes in length, based on a biblical text, presented with an awareness of both the seasons of the Church Year and the realities of the contemporary context.

"Homily" has variously meant something shorter in length than a sermon. Traditionally it has referred to such things as "a conversation," "meditation," or moving through a biblical text verse-by-verse. It is sometimes used to refer to preaching that happens on special occasions, such as at funerals or weddings.

The mystery of preaching

Can Jesus' question provide some perspective on life that might keep the way open for further discussion, new insights, the heightening and deepening of faith? Yes! For the homiletical journey always provides both tangible experience and divine mystery. Note how the apostle Paul refers to this mystery in the fourth chapter of Colossians. Here he asks his listeners for their prayers while he is in prison "that God will open to us a door for the word, that we may declare the mystery of Christ" (Colossians 4:3).

Mystery! It is no accident that some of the world's most interesting theological writers have also been mystery writers.[3] Jesus' question tips us off to the fact that he is posing a *mystery* for us. His is the question and ours is the homiletical adventure to pursue. How will our preaching be faithful to the mystery of Jesus Christ and God's love in the postmodern context? His mysterious question encourages proclamation to bind together those who are always learning to love with the one who loves, the person of Jesus Christ.

Jesus asked a lot of questions he did not answer. The mighty witnesses of the biblical story are a magnificent effort to tangle with the God identity question. As we consider preaching in today's context, how can we look at the reality of Jesus Christ and the gospel in a way that leaves Jesus' question a question and that allows the mysteries of our faith some root room to flourish? To honor preaching as mystery, this book is about directions, possibilities, and exploration. It is not intended to provide one single and complete homiletical and theological answer. But it is intent on inviting attention to the mysterious love of God in our lives, and the way we hear that in our Lutheran preaching.

Rather than shy away from the problematic multiple views of reality and truth presented to Christians in a postmodern setting, we can take our cue from Jesus' question and approach it with the zest of those who are profoundly curious about 'whodunit' and why.

It is mystery in the best sense, not only that which bids us figure out things but also encourages us to enjoy the wonder, the hiddenness, and the promises that beckon us.

For reflection

1. How is the person of Jesus Christ described in the preaching you hear? His personhood? His deeds?
2. Why do you think Jesus' question, "Who do you say that I am?" has caused so much comment over the centuries? How do you answer the question in your life?
3. Does the preaching you hear, or do, reflect the invitational nature of Jesus' question? How do you hear or speak of the question of Jesus' identity in preaching?
4. Using the chapter's definition of "postmodern," what would you say is the biggest challenge for preaching in the "postmodern" world? What would be the characteristics of good postmodern preaching in your view?

1

The "Lutheran" in Lutheran Preaching

"How beautiful upon the mountains are the feet of the messenger who announces peace, who brings good news, who announces salvation, who says to Zion, 'Your God reigns.'"

⌘ *Isaiah 52:7*

In almost all geographical areas of the Evangelical Lutheran Church in America (ELCA), congregations, when asked to fill out materials for a new pastoral search, almost inevitably list as their first priority in pastoral leadership the ministry of preaching. From the fiery pulpit rhetoric of Luther to the widely assorted tones and moods of Lutheran preachers today, preaching, whether one is laity or ordained, has been at the core of what it means to define one's identity as a Lutheran. So, what are the characteristics of a Lutheran sermon?

This chapter will respond to that question first by looking at how preaching defined as "Lutheran" developed out of the actual preaching work of the Reformation and how that was reflected theoretically in its confessional documents. Next, we will look at what overall types of expectations and experiences Lutherans have had as preachers and listeners to the preaching event. Third, we will assess the recent changes over the last century that are influencing contemporary Lutheran preaching. Finally, given these changes, we will look at significant challenges now facing Lutheran preaching in its next Spirit-led steps in a postmodern world.

Reformation and preaching

The Reformation principle for preaching was very clear and simple:

> To preach means to convey the content of the Scriptures to listeners, to say that which the Bible itself is saying. God speaks in the Bible, and when the Bible is proclaimed and God speaks to men [sic] from the pulpit, God's Word is Christ. So when the gospel sounds forth it is the living Christ come down among men [sic] who listen in faith.[1]

How do modern-day sermon listeners respond to this Reformation understanding of preaching? Would they credit preaching with this type of authority? Would they agree on choice of topics?

The role of the laity listeners? Clearly it represents a very high and lofty view of the preaching task. It follows a hierarchy of expression beginning with God, through Christ via the Bible through the work of the preacher and finally into the ears of the listeners.

How did this view of preaching evolve from the turmoil of the Reformation, which created many new directions in preaching? The pulpit became the focus of the reforming efforts of the sixteenth century leaders and, as a result, the forms and intentions of preaching underwent significant changes from the late medieval preaching of the era Luther inherited as a young monk.

These changes took place in several areas, including the role of preaching in relation to the overall worship service, use of the Bible, topics preached, and the educational needs preaching fulfilled. By its very nature, Reformation pulpit rhetoric served to create and sustain a movement of reform that was reiterated in the hearing of the common people on a regular weekly, and sometimes even daily, schedule.

At its core, the reformation of preaching emphasized a loving and gracious God and freedom in Christ from both unlawful spiritual and earthly constraints. Over time, Lutheran proclamation spelled out more clearly the blessed tensions of human life and God's activities by naming the paradoxes and core affirmations of the Christian faith as reflected from the Bible. Some of these faith dynamics are well known among Lutheran sermon listeners: law and gospel, sinner yet saint, saved by grace through faith, and the priesthood of all believers.

The needs of the newly reforming Church movement were many. And while preaching was central to the work of the Reformation, the time to analyze and write about preaching theory never happened in any uniform way. Luther threatened to write a preaching manual because of the poor preaching he consistently heard, but he never actually found the time. Melanchthon, lay person and scholar of the Reformation, wrote extensively on rhetoric, even ascribing to preaching a special type of rhetoric as instructional and didactic in nature.

Yet, Melanchthon also found no opportunity to write at length on preaching. Although he was a layperson and educator, he nevertheless did preach on occasion. His sermon at Luther's final funeral service—three were held—is a scholarly, loving, and elegant piece of pulpit rhetoric that honors the very best of the scholarly impulses of the Reformation.[2]

Evidences of what came to be called "Lutheran preaching" were already evident in published sermons and in some of the confessional documents contained in *The Book of Concord*.[3] Luther's contributions to this collection were minor in number, but one statement in particular is significant for his description of preaching. The statement sums up his understanding of the gospel and its primary vehicle of expression. In the "Smalkald Articles," he says:

> We now return to the gospel, which gives guidance and help against sin in more than one way, because God is extravagantly rich in his grace: first, through the spoken word, in which the forgiveness of sins is preached to the whole world (which is the proper function of the gospel); second, through baptism; third, through the holy Sacrament of the Altar; fourth, through the power of the keys, and also through the mutual conversation and consolation of brothers and sisters. Matthew 18 [:20]: "Where two or three are gathered . . ."[4]

This particular article has come to be known in its entirety by the phrase "Means of Grace."[5] It is significant that all of these means of experiencing God's gracious activity in human life are mediated by language. Thus, for Luther the premier means of grace is God speaking through the act of preaching. It is this view of preaching that has earmarked proclamation as unique for Lutherans.

Other expressions of preaching also emerged in the Reformation. Luther produced a number of what were called "postilla."[6] These postilla were a form of today's lectionary sermon aids and offered the preacher a vast number of insights into a lectionary text. Luther was frustrated by the fact that some preachers used these "postilla" word-for-word as their own Sunday sermons! Yet, he was even more dismayed by those who ignored them, and he pointedly ridiculed such preachers in his own pithy way:

> Everything that they are to teach and preach is now so very clearly and easily presented in so many salutary books, which truly deliver what the other manuals promised in their titles: "Sermons That Preach Themselves," "Sleep Soundly," "Be Prepared," and "Thesaurus." Yet, they are not upright and honest enough to buy such books, or, if they have them already, to consult or read them. Oh, these shameful gluttons and servants of their bellies are better suited to be swineherds and keepers of dogs than guardians of souls and pastors.[7]

Other sources of Reformation literature that spoke of preaching, were Luther's varied observations on preaching found in the American edition of Luther's *Table Talk*.[8] A look at the index will provide a rich list of quotes, quips, and barbed remarks that Luther made to his table companions on preaching and sermons!

Other sources include translated sermons in the American Edition of Luther's Works[9] and the eight volume series of translated sermons by Lenker.[10] References to the act and meaning of preaching are sometimes embedded within sermons themselves, and there are frequent references to preaching found in other types of materials Luther produced.[11]

One of the sermonic remarks that reflects on the importance of preaching is found at the conclusion of one of Luther's sermons on the Gospel of John. He was obviously in a cranky mood that day, but certainly made his point as to why listeners ought to "listen up!"

> Well, so far as I am concerned, you need not mend your ways. I shall not yield, and you also will not yield. But on the Day of Judgment God will ask me: "Did you preach that?" and I will be able to say yes. Then He will turn to you with the question: "Did you hear that sermon?" and you will answer yes. And in reply to God's next question to you: "Why then did you not believe it?" you will say: "Oh, I took it to be the mere word of man, spoken by a poor chaplain or village pastor!" And now this Word, implanted in your heart, will accuse you and be your accuser and judge on the Last Day."[12]

Our picture of preaching in the Reformation remains limited, however. No major studies have been done of it because of the linguistic problems presented by the changes in the German language at that time. It is also evident from the overall massive collection of sermons found in the Weimar edition of Luther's works[13] that only a very small number of his sermons have been translated into English. Lacking any Reformation era treatise on preaching, descriptions of it must be derived historically from the sermons themselves or the sporadic references to preaching in the confessional documents of the era.

Today's Lutheran preaching

Given this richly varied material, what seems to have evolved as a "typical Lutheran sermon" for most preachers and listeners today? The answer depends on the setting and types of preachers people have experienced. For those who are lifelong Lutherans, description of a sermon may be easy. However, many people in Lutheran faith settings today might have experienced many different types of preaching. Many may have expectations that present a radical departure from the traditional views of the Lutheran sermon constructs and moods heard in Lutheran settings today. Undoubtedly, one of the gifts of the Lutheran Christian faith perspective is a strong emphasis on preaching and the Bible, and so one might *generally* characterize a Lutheran sermon as:

- Liturgical—that is, it makes connections explicitly and implicitly with the rest of the worship service, including the sacraments.
- Interactive with biblical texts on a regular basis.
- Reflecting regularly on the relationships between the divine, the human, and the world.
- Expressive of the lived Christian tension between God's law and God's gospel.
- Utilizing a variety of forms and methods of presentation.
- Preaching done by either an ordained or lay person, female or male.
- Seeking application of texts and ideas to contemporary lived life.
- A long-term means of forming a congregation's spirituality.
- Highly susceptible to influences of societal uses of language.
- Speaking obliquely about social issues, although it does assert the tension between a pastoral and prophetic way of speaking.
- Prepared—that is, the doctrine of inspiration underlying Lutheran sermons is not focused on a charismatic, stream-of-consciousness mode of delivery, but depends on the thoughtful preparation of the preacher beforehand.

It is obvious that Lutherans and listeners to Lutheran sermons have had experiences that depart radically from this list. In some ways, this is typical due to the ongoing changes in preaching in all times and places. However, in describing Lutheran proclamation as a distinctive type of preaching that has evolved over the last several centuries, it is also possible to note that anything called a "Lutheran sermon" does not or should not contain certain elements.

So, Lutheran preaching is (hopefully) characterized by not being:

- a speech;
- a lecture on the Bible;
- moralizing;
- a personal platform for social issues;

- aimed only at the individual listener (note the importance of the corporate dimension of the faith);
- a clergy means of "getting even" or preaching on favored topics repeatedly;
- lacking the personal witness of the preacher;
- repeated (except under major emergency circumstance!);
- prejudiced in ethnic, gender, age, or class terms;
- irrelevant to the lives and questions of the listeners.

What is different today about Lutheran proclamation?

Whatever the historical or inherited expectations of the sermon Lutherans might have, as listening Lutherans we are always being formed by new elements and challenges in preaching. What factors today show the changes Lutheran proclamation has undergone since the first few decades of the Reformation era?

First, the *setting* of preaching has shifted significantly from the center of worship life to being one of several elements a worshiper encounters on a Sunday morning. The last thirty years in particular have placed preaching within the larger context of worship.[14] One will find, for example, an ELCA national church office called "Worship" with preaching understood as part of that designation. There are many reasons for this, including a reappraisal of the role of the sacraments, a deeper valuation of the meaning and impact of context, a wider appeal to the senses in worship beyond that of only hearing and seeing, the influence of ecumenical ties, the disappearance of the "great preachers" model of the first half of the 20th Century, and the increase in multiple sources of information and inspiration.

Another change in preaching has to do with the ethos, or character, of the one preaching. This has changed in several ways. First, since the ordination of women in the Lutheran Church in 1970, both women and men now preach regularly in the ELCA. This has greatly affected preaching given the different gendered experiences, perceptions, and theological approaches each sex brings to the pulpit. While listeners will hear, see, and feel different responses to the preaching of men and women, unfortunately, the study of this phenomenon in the Church is rare and little information exists at this point to document how and in what way preaching has been affected.[15] Sadly, there are still congregations who are resistant to the gifts of preaching that women can bring to the pulpit.

Another difference in the pulpit that more and more faith communities are observing is an increased of laity preaching. This phenomenon is due to the current shortage of available ordained persons, the respect accorded to demonstrated lay leadership skills in this area, and a long tradition of lay preaching in the church. This tradition is sometimes seen in the "temple talks" parish members give on a specific topic such as stewardship or the sermon a lay person may preach when substituting for the pastor who is unavailable.

Laity presence in the pulpit is treated differently in various regions of the church. In some areas, regularly scheduled lay schools function under the aegis of a synod office. There are also a variety of educational programs offered to laity who exhibit leadership and preaching skills in their local settings. In other areas, lay preachers are not permitted, except on an only infrequent basis. How are we to regard this challenge now? Is it a temporary reality, or is the church now being asked to reassess the ancient meaning of preaching? Is it to be seen as another of the "tent-making ministries" that more heavily involve lay leadership? And how may it be connected with the increased need to do evangelism based on personal witness, regardless of lay or ordained status? Given the pressures of financial realities, leadership availability, and ongoing theological discussions about the role of clergy and laity in the church, the question of what the future of preaching holds could be interesting indeed.

One area of preaching that has changed significantly is the way in which some of the larger, traditional Lutheran theological concerns are now addressed. Given the Lutheran penchant for holding opposites in tension, paradoxical phrases such as law/gospel, justification/sanctification, sinner/yet saint, faith/works are often described in diffuse ways by utilizing different vocabulary, images, and stories (biblical or nonbiblical). For example, the naming of sin, including the word itself, is described in more existentialist, psychological, or nontheological words. Whether this blunts or dismantles the meanings of this and other theologically loaded terms is both a communication and theological issue open to debate.

Listeners also hear the Bible in ways that their Reformation forbears never did. Bible now is read and heard primarily by means of lectionary in most faith communities. Lectionary cycles may have been in effect even in biblical times,[16] but the selections offered now represent communities beyond Lutherans, yielding a potentially broad ecumenical flavor to worship. Lectionary readings have become commercialized to such an extent that preaching preparations are related to a vast market of Internet and published resources. The lectionary is tied very closely to what is called the Church Year, which moves through the cycles of the life, death, and resurrection of Jesus Christ.

With such a strong sense of the need to preach only from the lectionary, preachers and congregations sometimes do not feel the freedom to do preaching that is not lectionary governed. Yet, Luther himself preached sermon series on occasion, calling them "row sermons." Sermon series are a refreshing change from the lectionary cycle and can be done during certain seasons of the year, using texts that are based on a theme or "preaching through" a book of the Bible.

In another area of change, more attention in homiletics instruction has been given to the sermon's function. In other words, what does the preacher want the sermon to *do*? What work should a sermon hopefully do in a congregation to create needed change? Here again the expectations of the function of the sermon vary as widely as the biblical text and context of the sermon. The sermon may variously inspire, challenge, berate, bless, question, exhort, educate, praise, and express gratitude. It is a fascinating exercise to look at a biblical text and then place it in a variety of settings to see how the function of the sermon might change from setting to setting.

The media for preaching has shown the widest number of changes. Unlike the high, lone pulpits of the Reformation era with the male, ordained preacher speaking, preaching today involves a complex array of persuasive means. Technology ranging from a microphone, a radio, tapes, or the Internet images used in a computer-projected presentation on a church wall change the dynamics of the person-to-person sense of preaching. Dialogue sermons, dramas, and the use of question-answer formats between preacher and listeners further change the more traditional preacher/listener dynamic. These forms of visual and auditory rhetoric have significant implications for the role, authority, and person of the preacher. The technological changes that bring an emphasis on the visual have encouraged an increase in the use of story and image in preaching in the last thirty years.

Preaching of a strictly abstractly theological nature is rarely heard in most congregations today. Why is this? Historically, preaching has been moving away from the abstract propositions of theology to other forms of sharing the faith. There has been a growing appreciation for more than the auditory in proclamation. Luther valued the role of *hearing* the gospel above all else. Part of the reason for this was based on his biblical views. He also saw the problems that an overemphasis on other sensory impressions might cause in worship. However, the sermon is using story and image more because cultural, educational, and theological reasons have yielded evidence of how learning and appropriation of the faith include what is seen and experienced, as well as what is heard.

Opportunities, directions, and tensions ahead

Where to next for Lutheran preaching in the twenty-first century? Several things are now on the horizon, and some have already arrived. The biggest challenge begins with the Christian community itself. In a postmodern world, it is increasingly obvious that the long-held methods of asserting truth claims about the Christian faith must rely on more than the reiteration of traditional views. Perhaps the most exciting and sometimes painful reality that presents itself to the household of faith is that preaching spoken and lived out must shift its assertions of "the truth" to include the very real matter of personal witness to Jesus Christ. It is only in the lived-out witnessing to the truth of Christ's reality, inspired by the work of the Spirit, that the world will see that the truth always arrives embodied in the lives of the preacher and of the listeners. For some reticent Lutherans, this is a big challenge!

Why is this the center of unfolding, new directions? Lutherans are increasingly aware of the need to be an evangelizing church, not simply to gain church members but as a response to the realization that people will not automatically "come to us " because of prior ethnic church ties or the self-evident truths of our faith. The preaching event is beginning to take up this challenge with more listener-friendly and culturally-aware means of preaching the gospel. Sermon forms are evolving that combine preaching and teaching, as many hear the gospel for the first time, often with no prior Christian instruction. Sometimes this is accompanied with the innovative uses of technology, time, and space. As always, there is constant need for theological evaluation of how these varied efforts serve the gospel.

One of the most interesting challenges to preaching today has to do with an increased awareness not only of ecumenical Christian faith neighbors but also of intrafaith dialogues and contacts. How can Lutheran preaching effectively speak about relationships with Christian and non-Christian neighbors? This is asking the preacher to put the gospel on the global screen and challenges the listeners to ask: What is truth? Is this the same as evangelism? How does the sermon frame a gospel in a world that has so many other voices asking for respect and consideration?

Finally, one of the words used often in the last ten years is that of "spirituality." It is a word that emerges primarily from the historical faith tributaries of the Roman Catholic Church, and thus from our own heritage as well. In other eras, attending to the spirituality of sermon listeners has been termed, homiletically, as "spiritual care," "the care of souls," or "pastoral care." There is a growing sense that the preaching event can be intentionally understood and used as a means of fostering individual and corporate spirituality. Preaching can move beyond a Sunday-by-Sunday short-term means of communicating the gospel to a view that appreciates the long-term intention of forming a people for God through the spiritual work of the sermon.

For reflection

1. What points would you add or change in the chapter's listing of what a Lutheran sermon is?
2. How much of the traditional vocabulary of Lutheran theology do you hear in Lutheran preaching?
3. How do you understand the role of the Bible in preaching?
4. What do you hope to hear in "a good sermon"?
5. Which changes in Lutheran proclamation of the last thirty years do you agree with? Affirm? Disagree with?
6. How do you view the current challenges to Lutheran proclamation? What are the growing edges? What concerns you?
7. What do you think are the differences between a sermon preached to lifelong Lutherans and one preached to someone new to the Christian faith?

2

"It's the Gospel Truth!" The Bible, Lectionary, and Preaching

"But there are also many other things that Jesus did; if every one of them were written down, I suppose the world itself could not contain the books that would be written."

♫ *John 21:25*

One of the most hilarious fictional episodes in American fiction related to the Bible is found in Mark Twain's fiction work, *Tom Sawyer*. The local congregation sponsors a contest for children that encourages them to memorize as many Bible verses as possible. For each verse memorized the child is given a ticket, and the one with the most tickets gets the prize. Tom swaps all sorts of things with his peers to accumulate tickets and win that prize. However, when he is called up in front of the crowd and is asked to recite a few verses, his ignorance is revealed and he runs off in embarrassment.

In some ways, this fictional episode is a reflection of the general role of the Bible in American culture today. While the Bible's presence, visibility, and perceived riches are of interest to many, how does that interest become something more? How do readers and listeners actually attest to the Bible's contents and message in some meaningful way?

As a "symbol" of the Christian faith, the Bible is seen everywhere—in hotel rooms, homes, hospitals, and other places of ministry. It is often carried in liturgical processions and held aloft by lay reader or pastor at the conclusion of a reading, followed by the proclamation, "The Word of the Lord." Sunday-by-Sunday excerpts of the Bible, called the lectionary, are read in worship and printed in many church bulletins each week. It is the rare tele-evangelist who does not carry, thump, or ruffle the pages of a Bible. As one preaching student told me, "The tele-evangelists taught me how to fluff up my Bible!" Its contents are vast and varied, and yet its import can be summed up in one verse—John 3:16—the favorite verse of sign-waving sports fans who try to grab the attention of television viewers.

The world's best selling book, the Bible is given as a gift at significant moments of a person's life. It is used in court settings to swear oaths, and its beginning pages might often carry the records of a family's births, marriages, and deaths. Words from the Bible are said at all significant religious moments in our lives, and its words permeate our liturgies and creeds. Scripture provides the text for thousands of pieces of sacred music. Political officials may quote its most well-known lines. In large cities and small towns alike, people debate with great intensity the legitimacy of the presence of biblical words. They argue about whether or not biblical words, such as the Ten Commandments, should appear in public courthouses, town squares, and school classrooms.

How do Lutherans actually "connect" with the Bible theologically? Spiritually? And in preaching? For many Lutherans, probably the first realization of Bible came in learning the popular Sunday School song, "Jesus Loves Me," the words following this statement being, "This I know, for the Bible tells me so."[1]

What did Bible mean to this Lutheran child growing up in a small Minnesota town in the 1950s and 60s? It meant a visible, well-used, and sometimes linguistically diverse book that formed the core of our religious education and worship experiences. Confirmation in high school was still marked in my home parish by an evening gathering in which the confirmands were seated in front of the congregation and quizzed on their religious and biblical knowledge. Each confirmation class was also assigned a Bible verse, and in our class picture the banner over us forty serious white-robed tenth graders reads from

Matthew's Gospel: "Go Ye Therefore . . ."

The preaching heard in our town's Lutheran parishes was always biblically based. And given the ethnic makeup and history of that small Minnesota town, the words of the Bible were also still spoken in Norwegian, Swedish, and German during special Holy Week services and an occasional funeral. One of the most significant gifts my congregation gave to its children was the realization of the centrality of the Bible.

Preaching and interpreting the Bible

For the Reformers, the very act of preaching is what constituted worship. Melanchthon asserts this in one of the most homiletically crucial statements in the Lutheran confessional documents of his time, when he says: "And yet the chief worship of God is to preach the gospel."[2] This statement means that preaching and the Bible form the definition of what it means to have worship—that liturgy alone without gospel read and preached is insufficient. The proclamation of the gospel, via the witness of the Bible, undergirds the principle activity of Christian worship.

However, the Reformers also understood that the act of preaching is not simply proclaiming the gospel of the good news in Jesus Christ directly from the pages of the Bible. This is so for two reasons. First, it is humanly impossible to preach "disinterestedly." Any preaching already is personal, channeled through the life words and person of the preacher, and it is also therefore an act of interpretation. There is no value-free place from which to preach! The preacher, the biblical passage, the setting or context, faith, beliefs, and forms of personal witness to the gospel all influence the way preaching happens, regardless of the extent to which people are aware of these multiple influences.

Secondly, while Lutheran preaching is intrinsically wrapped around the Bible and most often follows the yearly pattern of the lectionary, preaching is more deeply biblical than the rhythms of the

Church Year attached to certain passages. In fact, the Bible is actually a map or pointer to an even more central reality, a type of interpretive crossroads. The key phrase for Lutherans in speaking of the Bible and understanding its place in our faith lives is the phrase "Word of God." This phrase includes the printed biblical texts, but also points to other manifestations of God's Word in our lives, the primary one being the incarnation of God's child, Jesus the Christ. It is this phrase that is the foundation of Lutheran biblical interpretation, sometimes referred to as "hermeneutics."

It is important to note that for all of Luther's reassessment and repositioning of the Bible in the middle of the Christian community, he never lost sight of the person of Jesus Christ as the fullest expression of the Word of God. That fact allowed for greater latitude in the selection of biblical passages and biblical interpretation then as it does for Lutheran preachers now. And it is at this juncture of interpretation that the Bible continues to be so crucial in Lutheran preaching.

Since Lutherans understand that the "Word of God" designates more than the Bible as an expression of God's intentions towards humanity, this opens the way to a whole range of rich interpretive possibilities. It is here we refocus again on Luther's views of the gospel in the Smalkald Articles, where God's gospel is "preached" through the event of proclamation, the Sacraments, the forgiving of sins, and faithful conversation among Christians.[3]

What are the implications of this? First, it means that Lutherans use the Bible in preaching with the realization that since it informs and is informed by other expressions of God's Word, it is a *contextualized* view of the Bible. Luther's translation of the Bible into the vernacular of his day, a happy coincidence with the invention of the printing press, squarely located the Bible in the lives of the ordinary person. Its thoughts, theologies, perspectives, commandments, and life-giving message were immediately accessible to anyone who could read and to all who could listen and understand. Its interpretive functions became accessible to the laity as well as the clergy. Luther's view of the Bible took seriously the priesthood of all believers as the context in which the Bible is preached, taught, debated. More voices, all voices, were invited to join in reading, speaking, living and debating the Bible.

However, Luther's writings over the years demonstrate that the Bible had ascendancy over all other resources or teaching on leading the Christian life. For some, this was a major insight and change. In a list of "lesser authorities" he included history, tradition, the lives of the saints, and the authority of the papacy. Luther's own preaching was biblically based, regardless of the issues or contexts in which he was speaking.

Bible and lectionary: Connections and differences?

In Lutheran faith communities, the Bible is usually placed on the reading lectern in a large-bound format and sometimes in the pulpit as well. In some cases, Lutheran congregations will actually have Bibles placed in the pew racks. As a means of educating parishioners to the riches of the Bible, listeners will be invited to find the biblical passages for themselves prior to their public reading.

Lutherans, however, do live with a dual understanding of what "Bible" means. For some it is the actual book of the Bible used in Sunday or personal worship. For others, Bible is filtered through the bulletin inserts that feature weekly lectionary selections from the Bible, which for some become a kind of "canon within a canon."[4] These selections are almost always taken from the *Revised Common Lectionary*.[5] This latest version of a lectionary cycle literally reflects an ongoing, centuries-old process of choosing biblical passages for each calendar year that highlight the life, death, and resurrection of Jesus.[6]

What are the principles of text choice reflected in the *Revised Common Lectionary* (RCL)? Since the person and acts of Jesus Christ pattern the types of preaching one might hear during the Church Year, there is a priority of preaching days, ranging from the "everyday" texts Sunday by Sunday to the highest ranking preaching days of all, the six "Major Festivals." These all are centered on the major events having to do with Jesus Christ and, in calendar order are: Epiphany, Easter, Ascension, Pentecost, Holy Trinity Sunday, and Christmas.[7]

The current cycle is three years in length and each year features, in order, one of the synoptic Gospels. The contents of the Gospel of John do not have their own year, but its passages are read almost in their entirety by placement around the Lent and Easter season. How and who and why these choices are made is complex, and based on ecumenical traditions that have their own rich history.

This arrangement helps foster the ecumenical unity of the church and makes it easier for all planning and participating in worship to trace the key realities of the Christian faith. It avoids the difficulties of the free choice of texts that may result in missing what is crucial about Jesus Christ's life and ministry and the problems associated with a preacher choosing "favorite texts" on a regular basis.

However, the use of the lectionary—any lectionary—has always been a matter of historical debate. Some branches of the Christian faith do not use a lectionary, preferring to rely on current events, the flow of congregational faith life, and a variety of different views of the Bible as rationale for choosing preaching texts.[8] This perspective intersects with two historical approaches to the reading of biblical texts in public worship, and each reflects the strengths and weaknesses of its own tradition. Today the common practice, reflected in the RCL, is something called *lectio selectiva,* a Latin phrase meaning a choice of different texts. The other practice is reading and preaching on an ongoing reading from a book of the Bible, a practice called *lectio continua.*

One of the benefits of lectionary usage is that it features issues of perennial concern, regardless of a preacher's preferences. The repetition of the key Bible texts in a three-year cycle provides solid base of biblical understanding for worshippers. And difficult texts are not avoided in the lectionary readings, meaning that preachers will be challenged to deal with and interpret "hard" texts. Congregational ears always grow alert when the Jesus' words on divorce are read or the story of the woman about to be stoned for adultery is told. Modern ears probably cringe a bit when they hear of the punishment that is in store for those who reject children or listen to Jesus' words of harsh judgment that awaits some on the last day. Parishioners who wonder what these difficult texts have to do with their lives will wait to hear how the preacher can connect this ancient difficult word with their current reality.

One of the drawbacks of the lectionary system is that preachers sometimes feel strictly bound historically to the lectionary and do not feel the freedom to use texts outside the appointed texts. Yet, Luther himself occasionally preached a sermon series (he called them "row sermons"). The sermon quotation from his preaching on John in the previous chapter is part of the row preaching he did when acting as an interim pastor for his friend Bugenhagen in Wittenberg. In some parishes, Advent, Lent, and some summer weeks lend themselves to such "row" preaching on a particular Bible book, or on a set of verses related to a particular topic.

Large sections and even some entire books of the Bible are not included in the RCL currently used in most Lutheran congregations. This means some topics, persons, and issues have been omitted by virtue of committee decisions about what is most helpful to the faith life of twenty-first century Christians. Biblical interpretation has, as a result, taken some interesting turns in the ears of those who have lived through several lectionary cycles or who have heard the Bible used on topics of interest in other venues, such as television programs. It is here that various interpretations of the Bible may be omitted from preaching that holds strictly to the lectionary readings.

For example, concerns and disagreements over the role of women in church leadership, debates on homosexuality, and many significant Old Testament passages on the use and stewardship of land are three areas generally omitted in the current the RCL. This is apparent when observing the RCL's index of verses.

Thus, the Bible in its totality becomes a matter of theological choice when dependent on the lectionary system Lutherans use or choose not to use. While some may disagree with this perspective, it also reasserts that the Word of God is found primarily and centrally in the person of Jesus Christ as the final arbiter of all things human and divine. It also asserts that those who make the decisions about the lectionary are cognizant of the changes Christians have experienced in many areas of life and faith. And finally, it allows the preacher the freedom to choose what she or he deems most helpful to fostering the faith life of the people in a given setting.

For reflection

1. How is the book of the Bible displayed and used in your congregation?
2. How has the Bible formed your faith life?
3. What things do you consider in your own personal interpretation of the Bible? How do these compare with the interpretations you hear preached?
4. Is the lectionary used in your congregation? Why or why not?
5. Do you think most Lutherans are aware of how the lectionary cycle is written and the purposes for which it is used?
7. Do your hear preaching that deals with the more "difficult" lectionary texts that are read in worship?
8. If you could change anything about the use of the Bible or lectionary in your congregation, what would it be?

3

The Life of a
Lutheran Sermon

"But how are they to call on one in whom they have not believed? And how are they to believe in one of whom they have never heard? And how are they to hear without someone to proclaim him?"

⇨ *Romans 10:14*

One of the more mysterious areas of a preacher's life has to do with sermon preparation. "Why do some preachers need to take an entire day to write a sermon?" a parishioner might ask. "When will I find the time I need to write a sermon?" the preacher wonders. What elements combine to produce the preaching most Lutherans hear each Sunday morning? And how are these elements the same or different from those special or "occasional" sermons such as one might hear at a funeral or a wedding?

What elements are non-negotiable, the "must have" of any sermon, and which are always fluid and susceptible to change? This chapter will try to answer these questions to the extent it is possible, given the fact that every sermon is unique. While a sermon might have much in common with others preached in a tradition of some faith community, each is also unlike any other before it or yet to come. Even a sermon repeated twice on the same Sunday morning at two different worship services is, as every preacher will tell you, really two different sermons. It is the same for sermons preached at funerals, weddings, confirmations, and baptisms—the same, yet different!

The sermon you hear preached is built on multiple layers—layers of history, tradition, Bible, congregation, preacher, listener, event, and season. All of these might be nuanced in different ways. But are there some commonalities each sermon shares? The answer is yes!

Sermonic "Basics"

It may come as a surprise to many that the craft and art of preaching is a form of sacred rhetoric common to almost all faith traditions, certainly to Christianity, Judaism, and Islam. Each of these members of this Abrahamic family of faith features preaching in some form. Obviously there are differences from one tradition to the next. These include sermon purpose, who is allowed to preach, the worship setting, the length, the topics, the intentions, and the sacred texts on which the sermons are developed. Yet, sacred rhetoric, preaching in the Christian tradition, has some very definable historical roots, that identify the "basics" needed for preaching. Christian proclamation has been built on the ancient Greek and Roman works in the field of rhetoric, the study and production of persuasive forms of speech. This history is rich and one upon which early Christian teachers and preachers drew. St. Augustine himself was a teacher of rhetoric prior to his conversion and wrote a book entitled *On Christian Doctrine.* This book is about biblical interpretation, and its final chapter is built on the rhetorical practices of Cicero. It provided rhetorical guidelines for the Christian preacher. Many Christian educators and preachers, Melanchthon and Luther both, were schooled in rhetoric and used its resources well. Early American Lutheran homiletics manuals that described the theories of preaching also were based on rhetorical practices that are over two thousand years old.[1]

Rhetoric and homiletics, however, are two areas of persuasive speech that have remained in tension. For example, rhetoric may be used to persuade anyone to do anything, however good or evil the purposes. Preaching has a more focused purpose of persuading listeners to believe in the message of the gospel of Jesus Christ, with all that means ethically. Thus, even in intentionality, subject matter, and goals preaching differs from rhetoric. However, the ancient rhetoricians did identity some basics in the act of speaking that are also true of the act of preaching. So, as with any rhetorical situation, in preaching we also need:

- a speaker/preacher
- words/content/subject matter
- listeners/audience/congregation
- context: where, when?

Given these primary elements, it is easy to see that they can combine and recombine in an almost endless array of possibilities. What if the speaker/preacher is a guest? A lay person? What if the listeners are children rather than adults? What if the preacher uses a theme from a biblical text rather than speaking on the text itself? It is here that we began to think of another layer of influences and demands that affect the preparation and preaching of a sermon.

The sermon variables

Parishioners might wonder how the preacher was trained at the seminary in the art of preparing a sermon! What are some of those elements that student preachers and "called" preachers need to consider in preparing a sermon? In the Lutheran tradition, there are several to consider, and if these are ignored or minimized, the preaching may lack meaning and relevance for the listeners. Here are some of the elements that Lutherans expect to hear in some fashion in preaching. These are not listed in order of importance.

Context/Setting—Each time a preacher prepares a sermon, he or she should ask the question: In what setting will this be proclaimed? Is this for Sunday morning or for a special service? Will it be in a church or a funeral home? Does the preaching space involve a pulpit or not?

Worship/Liturgy—While this can also be considered part of the overall reality of context, it does have its own special considerations. Is this a Lutheran worship service? Is it ecumenical? Is a sacrament being celebrated during this particular worship? How will the length of the liturgical part of the service affect the length of the sermon? What connections do the worship service and the sermon make with one another? Will the sermon "stand out" and even be counter to the worship, and if so, why?[2]

Bible—Is the text a regularly assigned lectionary text? Is it specially chosen for a particular Sunday or day? What translation of the Bible will be used? How much of a biblical text should be read and preached on? Is the text familiar or unfamiliar?

Big Ticket Events—What impact may unplanned, unexpected congregation-wide, national, or international events have on the lives of the listeners? A sermon preached on an assigned text for the Sunday that ignores the fact a parishioner died that morning or that war broke out two days earlier in the Middle East is exhibiting a sense of detachment from reality and poor pastoral-homiletical care for the listeners.

Theology—How does the preacher speak of what is happening in any given biblical text? If the text is about the birth of Jesus, does the preacher share something pertinent of the centuries of Christian thought on the topic of the Incarnation? If the Sunday is Holy Trinity Sunday, can the preacher blend the thoughts of faith with the poetry of its mysteries? Do the listeners hear in the preacher's sermons the theology, poetry, and resources that the greatest theological minds of all the centuries have pondered?

The Preacher—Who is preaching, and how does that affect proclamation? This is a crucial question when parishioners are used to one type of preacher and find that the one they are about to hear might be of a different ethnic group, sex, background, and theological persuasion. The persona or "ethos" of the preacher is also doubly critical, because the Bible models true proclamation as a form of public witness to one's own faith.

The Listeners—Odd as it sounds, listeners may sometimes be left out of the equation in planning a sermon! It is not enough to identify the Sunday's lectionary text and generally "aim it" at listeners. Who in the congregation has a particular need that might be targeted by a fresh new word? Luther once made this pithy remark about a fellow preacher sent out to preach at a senior care center of his own day:

One should preach about things that are suited to a given place and given persons. A preacher once preached that it's wicked for a woman to have a wet nurse for her child, and he devoted his whole sermon to a treatment of this matter although he had nothing but poor spinning women in his parish to whom such an admonition didn't apply. Similar was the preacher, who gave an exhortation in praise of marriage when he preached to some aged women in an infirmary.[3]

Sermonic Form and Intention—Every sermon is different because each comes with different forms, approaches, and intentions, no matter how subtle or explicit these might be. Every sermon is affected by what the preacher chooses to speak about. Will it be a specific part of the biblical text? Will it be a theme in the text? Will the entire text be preached? But identifying the intention of a sermon is only the first half of the preacher's work, because the preacher must always ask, "What is my intention in preaching this for the listeners?" Does this preacher wish the listeners to repent? praise? reflect? question? feel motivated enough to do evangelism? The more focused the preacher can be with form, selection, and intention, the more clear will listeners be about the question: "Where is this sermon going anyway?"

"Other" Resources—Sermon listeners and preachers are situated in several cultural and societal contexts. American and ethnic realities and values, the parish, the town, the school, the work environment, forms of media and entertainment, and local traditions all affect the lives of the listeners. How can the preacher take these strands of cultures into account in proclamation without violating the gospel or discounting people's daily experiences? How, for example, does one preach on the "Hallmark Card" days, such as Mother's Day, and yet remain true to the biblical witness, a witness that may even run counter to cultural experiences? Can the preacher effectively refer to movies, plays, sports events, and make the sermons live as a result?

By way of example

This list is essential in considering the elements that contribute to an effective sermon, yet one that is all-important in sharing the good news of God in Jesus Christ. How does such a list match up with an actual sermon? Following is a test case sermon that invites the reader to see to what extent the concerns of sermon-making apply to an actual sermon. The "For Reflection" questions will invite you to look at how this sermon was prepared.

This sermon is an "occasional sermon" I preached in November 2002 at the ordination of Fredrica Meitzen in the Gettysburg Lutheran Seminary's Chapel of the Abiding Presence. Read the Bible texts and the sermon. Then look at the analysis of it, which I apply to my own preaching.

Sermon on the Ordination of Fredrica Meitzen

Texts: Isaiah 58:6-9; Psalm 103:1-12, 21-22; Romans 12:4-8; John 13:12-17, 20

What a day this is! Fredrica, we are pleased and honored to be here this day, to celebrate your ordination into the ministry of Christ's church. Welcome to you all who have come to participate: this whole lively crew of folks from West Virginia, members of the Zion Etters congregation, Trinity Lutheran of Danville, Bishop Hendrix and rostered leaders of this synod, seminary community. In Christ's name, we welcome you!

Frederica, when I read the Gospel text for this day, I must admit my first response was "Oh, no. Not this text!" Not this messy, strange, frankly uncomfortable text describing an incident that is, well, some-how embarrassing. I originally hail from Lake Woebegone country myself, and believe me, Lutherans don't much talk about foot washing there. Except for the occasionally wise and brave congregation, they also regularly and happily omit it from their Maundy Thursday liturgies.

But here it is—right in the middle of John's Gospel. In fact, so important does John consider Jesus' action that we have a good half of the Chapter 13 given over to describing how and why he washed the feet of the disciples. The event of foot washing that John records is unique only to this Gospel and occurs in that last meal gathering of the disciples. Since this same Gospel offers no description of a communion narrative as part of the gathering, some faith communities name Jesus' action as the first sacrament, and some faith traditions practice it regularly as part of their worship life.

For us? Our churches, seminaries, offices, and Sunday schools are full of representations of many primary images from Jesus' ministry: out on the Galilean hills, by the lake, in the Garden. There are well-known depictions of the Last Supper by Leonardo da Vinci or Salvador Dali. But you will look in vain for any well-known and treasured picture of Jesus kneeling at the feet of his disciples and washing those feet. You will not find this a popular subject of many stained-glass windows. While the deaconess communities have valued this symbol, it is often a little noticed one. Who wants a picture of Jesus kneeling on the floor, washing feet, when he should be, excuse me, sitting at the head of the table, acting more lordly, more god-like?

There is *such* a "contextual messiness" about all of this that we can totally sympathize with Peter who loudly protests what Jesus is about to do for him, saying, "Lord, you are going to wash MY feet?"

This is an act we want to clean up, make more sanitary, less embarrassing so we can assign some theological meaning in such a way as to distance it from us. We are privileged to have as one of our instructors here, Dr. Warren Eshbach of the Church of the Brethren tradition. He tells the story of a pastor from another protestant tradition that very infrequently did this kind of thing, who came to him to borrow the traditional container for washing feet so this could be used at their Maundy Thursday services. The pastor was stunned to receive from Warren not a silver-plated basin, or even the charming and rustic wooden bucket that had been used and which had finally seen its day. Instead, Warren handed the pastor what they do use—a very large Tupperware container! Tupperware and Maundy Thursday worship—can we hold the thought of these two together?

That Jesus takes the normal duty of a household servant and transforms it into a picture of the way we are invited to do ministry with one another is the picture we share and ponder on this ordination day!

What were the disciples thinking as their teacher knelt before them, acting like a common servant? Except for Peter's outburst, we have no words recorded for this event, no other responses from anyone. Did any of them talk to him or to each other about what was happening? Did they acknowledge an action that was probably making them just as uncomfortable, curious, and embarrassed as mouthy Peter? We do not know. This was a nonverbal act of ministry on Jesus' part. It gives us pause, for we live in and minister in a very word-oriented and sometimes word-overwhelmed tradition, and yet this is the model of ministry Jesus demonstrates for the disciples in his final hours.

What was Jesus thinking and feeling as he knelt before each of the disciples, washing each pair of feet? Was he remembering that someone had done this very same act of service and love for him but days before? For John tells us in the previous chapter that "Mary took a pound of costly perfume made of pure nard, anointed Jesus' feet and wiped them with her hair" (12:3). It is something he could not have forgotten as he repeated the same action for his disciples. Did Jesus reflect on the long hours of walking and talking as he made his way around the room? Did he think about those group conflicts so typical of any group, those group joys and sorrows so typical of any band of God's followers?

So what do we make of this act of Jesus? Certainly it was symbolic, but also a concrete, enfleshed call to live out the heart of ministry with this model of service. For as Jesus returns to the table after washing everyone's feet he says quite succinctly in verse 15: "For I have set you an example, that you also should do as I have done to you." Here we do not have a Savior who is a "Don't do as I do but do as I say" God. We have one who shows us the loving manner and attitude in which ministry flows. And so we ask. *What does that look like*? What is our response to this act of Jesus if we choose to receive it and engage in it?

The responses to this incarnational act of love and service are just as concrete, just as contextual, just as real for all of us as Isaiah's words for today, spell them out clearly—acts of justice, redemption, welcome, and the easing of pain, suffering, and oppression. And one need look no further than the communities in which we live to find these needs and these imperatives of God who calls us to attend to them. It is one thing to start with those familiar projects of faith and service to which we are called, but Isaiah shows that an even more consistent and deeper way of practicing all of our Christian spirituality requires us to engage in both daily attitudes of justice thinking and daily acts of justice doing for Christ's sake.

One of the familiar prayers of our liturgy gives thanks at the end of the service to God who gives us his Jesus as a "model of the godly life." The prayer also asks that we be enabled to "conform our lives to us." Jesus' example in today's Gospel shows us what the model of the godly life is about.

This past week as I shared this text with others and we talked about it, one new pastor in the Pittsburgh area told me what the experience of washing his parishioners' feet was like last Lenten season. First, he said, his people told him that they had felt very vulnerable as they participated in this act. He said he did, too, because as he knelt to wash each person's feet, he saw both his face and the other person's reflected in the waters, linked in Christ's name in love and service, just as we might see our faces reflected in the water of the baptismal font.

So on this ordination day we give thanks for our God, for Jesus Christ, the washer of feet, the One who calls to ministry and blesses it with his presence and example. We have with us always, first of all, the Lord who ministers to each of us; who acts towards us with gentleness and thoughtfulness; who teaches us by example in our own lives what we are called to do in the lives of others. The first conversation for good and justice-filled ministry always begins between our God and us. And it is important that it began there, for we also then are able to see something else beyond the foot washing—just as Jesus did—to see the reality of true ministry. We will be able to see the crossroads of all words and deeds of ministry and love. We will see the cross.

In all our efforts of discipleship—whether successful or not— in any community of faith, in all those interactions among God's people, and people and their pastor, *there is always the Cross in it.* The Cross, our meeting place, our ministering place, our healing place, the site of forgiveness and renewal, and the source of empowerment.

Fredrica, people of the Etters congregation, all friends here today: Our God, our mentor Savior, is not only calling us to what we are to do, but showing us. . . . As you and your congregation engage in ministry for the sake of church and the world, may your joy, your struggles, your work for the gospel be done in the name of the One who calls us to ministry in word and in loving deed with joy and thanksgiving.

Amen!

For reflection

1. How can a sermon be said to "have a life of its own"?
2. Review the list of variables in a sermon. Which variable(s) is/are more important to you when preaching or listening to a sermon? Which of the variables seem to be emphasized in your local worship settings? Which are omitted or minimized?
3. How do you hear "the basics" of the preaching event emphasized in your congregation?

For reflection on the sermon

1. What is the context for this sermon, and in what ways does it differ from assigned lectionary preaching on an "ordinary" Sunday morning?
2. How would you describe the form of the sermon?
3. What do you think the preacher's main intention is in this sermon?
4. What is the preacher doing with biblical materials used?
5. What does the sermon say about liturgy?
6. What theological realities does the sermon raise for the listeners?
7. What attitude does the preacher express towards the listeners?

4

The Pulpit: A Look at the Preaching Furniture

*"Cold Spring Granite in Minnesota, for example, offers a granite pul-
pit. Granite makes a statement that no other material does."*

  ◁▷ *Jim Rausch of Cold Spring Granite.* [1]

In the early American fiction classic, *Moby Dick,* there is a stun-
ning description of a seaside chapel and its pulpit. The builders of
the chapel, men of the sea, had managed to convey the sense of the
pulpit as part of an actual ship. To ascend the pulpit, the preacher
had to climb a rope ladder as though climbing the mast. With the
backdrop of a picture of a ship at sea, Melville concludes the chapter
entitled "The Pulpit" with this dramatic statement: "What could be
more full of meaning?—for the pulpit is ever this earth's foremost part. .
. .Yes, the world's a ship on its passage out, and not a voyage complete; and the pulpit is the prow."[2]

The event of preaching has always been connected with the pulpit, and as Melville's insight shows, it is indeed a place of many
meanings. What exactly is a pulpit? The answer is twofold: pulpits
might be described in concrete, historical, and architectural terms,
and in theoretical ways. The word "pulpit" is derived from the Latin
Pulpitum, which means "a scaffold, stage, platform."[3] Through the
ages pulpits have been fashioned from all sorts of materials—marble
or granite, wood and metal, and artificial materials.

The architectural history of pulpits is not simply a matter of the
materials used in their production. Rather these and all pulpits demonstrate their own particular "rhetoric of architecture" which informs the
onlooker of what types of verbal rhetoric they host. Just as words persuade, so also do the visual representations of any given pulpit.

The evolution of the pulpit

Biblically, some scant evidence exists for the relationship between preaching and the artifacts used to support it. In Luke 4:16-20, we have a description of Jesus' reading Scripture and preaching on it. Verse 16 notes that "He stood up to read." And after he concludes reading the Isaiah text, the Gospel writer then says in verses 20, 21 that "he rolled up the scroll, gave it back to the attendant, and sat down. . . . Then he began to say to them . . ." Here, we can surmise there might have been a reading table on which to place the scroll, but the event of preaching took place with Jesus seated. Despite this description of more relaxed preaching posture, the obvious impact of Jesus' words almost resulted in his murder.

The fact that Jesus sat down to preach was also reflected in the earliest developments of a chair for the bishop to use when addressing a congregation, *ex cathedra*—"from the chair." Archeological evidence exists that pulpits were created outside from already existing community meeting places that had significant stone formations which could be used as a pulpit. An example of a magnificent stone pulpit, used by John Chrysostom, can be seen in the city of Istanbul.

The evolution of the pulpit was also related to something called an "ambo," or raised platform, from which lessons and part of the liturgy might be spoken or chanted. Some churches had double-decker or even triple-decker forms of this particular kind of chancel furniture. These types reflected the worship and preaching theologies of any given era and denomination.[4]

The building materials, the setting, height, width, and placement in the worship space (if at all today), all contribute to supporting the kind of homiletical rhetoric the listener might expect to hear. It is interesting to consider in what ways the design of the pulpit and the preacher's speech mutually enhance and support one another.

Conversely, pulpit architecture may actually contradict or hinder the preaching style. In the 1990s, for example, at Gettysburg

Lutheran Seminary a donated pulpit and altar were used for a time in the preaching practicum sessions. The old pulpit was constructed in a way that hampered human movement and could not be adjusted for reading table height. Its beautiful wood and imposing structure actually became the source of on-going complaints from students, whose preaching styles were evolving toward freer movement and a more contemporary "look" to proclamation. What had worked well for their grandparents' church setting was not working for them at all in their day.

In the mid-20th Century Midwest, I experienced pulpits that were often enhanced by lighting, almost a type of stage production. I observed, and then later experienced as a supply preacher, that once the pastor stepped into the pulpit, the lights were dimmed. While the focus was definitely on the preacher, it almost seemed conducive to nap time!

Whether one is the preacher or listening to preaching, it is interesting to consider the wide array of pulpit types from which the Word of God is proclaimed. Today, some worship spaces still use the older 20th and even 19th century pulpits. These are often massive, impressive, and nonadjustable. The preacher's body is usually visible only from the waist and, in some cases, the chest on up. These kinds of pulpits are often set high above the congregation and have a series of steps the preacher must ascend. The reading lamp in some of these older pulpits is probably there to offset the darkness caused by the dimming of the lights in the past, or added as an enhancement to inadequate chancel lighting.

More contemporary pulpits are sometimes constructed in such a way as to resemble the smaller, simple lectern. In some congregations the lectern and the pulpit have been combined into one piece of furniture. As a result, some of these pulpits are constructed so that the preacher's entire body is seen and there is less visible physical constraint. In some parishes there is a debatable use of the altar as the preaching place, an interesting merging—or confusing—of the traditional Lutheran emphasis on "Word and Sacraments."

Finally, in some settings the pulpit has either been removed altogether or is not used. The preacher walks around the chancel area or combines that with speaking and walking among the listeners in the worship area. This is a style many tele-evangelists use, where the focus is on the person speaking with no pulpit present. Such a style has the potential for making some people uncomfortable who expect the preacher and people to remain a comfortable distance apart. On the other hand, such freedom of movement between preacher and people may signify a return to more ancient forms of speaking that did not include the intermediary of furniture. There is actually a field of study called "proxemics," that studies how space is utilized, including such matters as how either distance or proximity might affect people's interactions with one another.

As many of us have learned, pulpits can be hazardous places for preaching, or at the very least come supplied with plenty of potentially distracting items—paraments, books, water glasses, paper, Bible, Kleenex, reading lamp (some have overly hot bulbs!), throat lozenges, and paper! One Sunday while supply preaching, I even encountered a small sealed vial of smelling salts for use when someone fainted! This assortment of items is probably not exactly what Melville had in mind in his description of the power of the pulpit.

The pulpit: theology, politics, community, and faith

What does a pulpit represent? It can be many things, depending on whom you ask. A symbol, a sign of authority, a barrier, a refuge, a utilitarian object, liturgical furniture, a political trajectory. Some hear God's Word preached from it while others hear human agendas discussed. It is probably the only piece of furniture that has had a plant named after it—a Jack-in-the-Pulpit![5]

For some it is the object of humor. You've probably heard people sarcastically remark that they wish their church's pulpit was equipped with a trapdoor. People periodically have disagreements over who has the right to stand in the pulpit and preach. Many a

Call Committee member can attest to that. And on certain unforgettable occasions, the pulpit may be remembered for being the place where a particular preacher denounced someone or something, revealed unsettling truths, or had the "last word."

National political debates have been waged in America's history. A large portrait that hangs in the Gettysburg Lutheran Seminary library pictures an American pastor in a Revolutionary Era pulpit removing his clerical robe to show the American army uniform he is wearing beneath it. In the sixties, pulpits became the setting for many a civil rights rallying cry.

There is a rich literature of sermons preached in northern and southern pulpits during the Civil War, debating the primary issues of that war from many vantage points. Sermons are also available from World War II, which do not dispute the war but rather provide preaching from those in prison or ministering in war-torn settings.[6] Sermons published on the Vietnam War, the Gulf War, the Iraqi War and "9/11," show the ways preachers have attempted to frame the Word of God in relationship to these times of political disturbance and war.

One of the more common phrases associated with the pulpit is "the bully pulpit." Interestingly, this phrase is from the early 20th Century and was coined by president Theodore Roosevelt who termed the White House a bully pulpit: "meaning a terrific platform from which to persuasively advocate an agenda."[7]

For whatever political purposes the pulpit has been used, there has and always will be a debate over the legitimacy of combining or separating concerns of faith and the world.

Hearing Jesus' question today

How do the pulpits (or lack of them) affect how we hear and respond to Jesus' question, "Who do you say that I am?" His question is one that invites us to come near. It is not an abstract question that we can answer at a distance. Because the witness of preaching is personal and immediate, any type of pulpit hindering the listener from hearing Jesus' question presents a problem. This is why today's preachers are examining more closely the necessity and placement of a pulpit for their preaching and their congregation's listening. Preachers and people are asking how the realities of space, acoustics, seating, congregational and pastoral relationships, and the incarnational nature of the preaching witness affect the decisions regarding a pulpit.

Obviously hearing Jesus' question is not simply a matter of pulpit furniture in and of itself. *Who* is in the pulpit makes a great deal of difference. Not all preachers are convinced they should be there and if they are, their forms of witness to the gospel vary greatly. Some can preach effectively from any pulpit, while others can only preach somewhat adequately if the furniture prevents them. Unfortunately, some preachers and some congregations welcome the pulpit as a barrier against each other and the gospel. The pulpit becomes a communal way of fending off relationships.

The *absence* of a pulpit has both advantages and disadvantages as well. Some listeners welcome the intimacy of a preacher who is able to stroll the seating area, gaze at them directly, and speak the gospel with a physical intimacy that no pulpit can allow. These listeners claim this style enables them to hear Jesus' question more clearly. But other listeners, for personal, theological, and historical reasons, shrink from what they perceive as the over-familiarity of the preacher. For them, such preaching represents an invasion of privacy rather than an invitation to community. It actually diminishes the thoughtful sense of Jesus' invitational question.

Clearly, the pulpit is not simply "furniture." It is the "holy" place where the life-giving gospel is proclaimed. That makes it an iconic, rhetorical, and physical reality that allows the listeners to see through the words and the place—to Jesus himself and to new life. How any given pulpit can mediate the preacher's words so the people hear Jesus' invitational question is something no faith community can take for granted.

For reflection

1. What type of pulpit does your faith community use?
2. What are the problems and advantages of this pulpit?
3. Has your worship setting abandoned the use of the pulpit and, if so, what advantages and disadvantages do you experience with preaching as a result?
4. How do you think the architectural rhetoric of your community's worship space, including the pulpit, functions?
5. Who should be allowed to use the pulpit in the life of your faith community? What restrictions would you place on who uses it, or what topics are discussed there?
6. How have you heard the combination, or separation, of faith and political life preached in your community?
7. Does the pulpit in your faith community enable you to hear clearly Jesus' question, "Who do you say that I am?" Why or why not?

5

Who's Preaching?
Who's Listening?

"Neither you or I could ever know anything about Christ, or believe him and receive him as Lord, unless these were offered to us and bestowed on our hearts through the preaching of the gospel by the Holy Spirit." [1]

  ❧ *Martin Luther*

At the usual Lutheran Sunday service, worship is intensely corporate. The rhythms of music, liturgy, prayers, and creeds involve the responses of those who are present. The words that are used in most of the worship service are available to the congregation through the bulletin—or perhaps bulletin inserts—the hymnal, and the Bibles in the pew racks. Added to these is the preaching event. With the exception of one speaker, everyone else is silent. Most are listening to what the preacher is saying, and what is said most likely is unscripted for the listeners beforehand.

What is happening here? What is the nature of preaching? The role of the listeners? What makes this proclamation event so distinctive within the worship service? Is this a form of communication that continues to be of any importance in today's culture and in a world that has widely diverse forms of information and versions of truth?

This chapter will examine the nature of the preacher/sermon listener relationship, as it has been traditionally understood. It will determine what has changed in that relationship in the later decades of the 20th century and which challenges this relationship faces today. While the sermon itself forms the "business" or the spine of the communication act, which is the center of the pastor/people relationship, we will explore what constitutes those critical *human relationships* that make it possible for the preacher to preach and the people to listen to that work of proclamation.

Preaching: Listener expectations

The Bible contains many stories about what happens between preachers and listeners. The prophets and Jesus all had the experience of being run out of town and even threatened with death when the listeners didn't like what they heard. Other communities rejoiced at the announcement of God's salvation and changed accordingly, even when the preacher was reluctant to see that happen (as in the story of Jonah). Preaching witnessed to and prompted the changes in the Pentecost community described in Acts. Listeners experienced preaching as the catapult that threw them into changed lives and new relationships. According to many biblical episodes, people left old commitments for new ones, repented, saw the evidence of God in their lives and, in turn, told other people about Jesus Christ through their own personal witness and proclamation.

The Book of Acts describes many interactions between preachers of the early days of Christianity and the listeners. Perhaps one of the most frightening, yet funny, episodes is described in the 20th chapter of Acts. It is one that many, many parishioners can identify with to some extent. The preacher is Paul, who "continued speaking until midnight" (v. 7). The time frame, however, didn't stop him! But what happens next did. "A young man named Eutyches, who was sitting in the window, began to sink into a deep sleep while Paul talked still longer" (v. 9). An open window ledge is not a good place to fall asleep. The young man falls out of the third story windowsill and dies. Paul interrupts his preaching, restores life to the young man, and then, says the writer (perhaps tongue-in-cheek), that "he [Paul] continued to converse with them until dawn; then he left" (v. 11). It is noteworthy that despite the late hour, the length of the sermon, and the death and resuscitation of a listener, preacher and people "hung in there" with one another through the night. Why?

What is it about preaching that keeps people listening? From a biblical perspective, preaching is the means to God's salvation. In the New Testament, preaching is considered fundamental to creating faith in Jesus Christ. This pattern of preaching people into faith, as a kind of spiritual midwifery, is specifically described in Romans, Chapter 10. Here we read a foundational view of not only the relationship preaching can create between God and a human being, but more specifically what this looks like between speaker and listener.

Paul describes this relationship between preacher and listener by pointing out that the gospel is "the word of faith that we proclaim" (v. 7). In the next verse he connects that proclaimed word with the listener, who will receive salvation "if you confess with your lips that Jesus is Lord and believe in your heart that God raised him from the dead." Paul says more about the faith relationship established between God and the listener. He then goes on to describe the role of the preacher in the people's salvation (vv. 14-17). The people will only hear God's salvation if there is a preacher to tell it. Paul concludes by saying, "So faith comes from what is heard, and what is heard comes through the word of Christ" (v. 17).

What does Paul's view of preaching, carried over into Lutheran theology, tell us about the specific traditional emphases in preaching, which characterize even today's Lutheran preaching events? He is saying that:

- Proclamation is a relational event—one which needs both preacher and listener.
- The preacher's role is central and not to be resisted, although some will.
- The relationship of preacher and listeners is initially auditory in nature for the listeners.
- The listeners' salvation is at stake.
- The result of preaching hopefully will be the listeners' confession of faith in Jesus Christ, prompted by the preacher's original confession of Christ in the act of proclamation. In other words,

the listener will move from listening to preaching to "speaking faith" in the same pattern as the preacher's.
• Given this pattern, preaching is both confessional and evangelistic in nature.

Lutheran preachers and listeners: A brief history

All of these factors laid the groundwork for the history of Christian proclamation and created the type of Lutheran preaching heard by most Lutherans on a Sunday morning. What has been established on preaching in historical Lutheranism in connection with Paul's statements on preaching? Luther certainly agreed with all that Paul noted about the preaching event. As the Reformation and its work continued over time, the act of preaching and the role of the listeners was repeatedly reassessed and given consideration in confessional documents that were created.

Melanchthon spelled out the relationship of people to preacher in terms of the struggle over what preachers choose as sermon topics and whether or not these nurture the listeners' spiritual well-being. It is the longest and most specific reference to preaching found in the confessional documents. Through his critique of preaching topics we read what Melanchthon considered essential for true preachers in order that they might elicit a positive salvific response from the listeners.

Among the opponents there are many regions where no sermons are delivered during the entire year except during Lent. And yet the chief worship of God is to preach the gospel. And when the opponents do preach, they talk about human traditions, about the devotion to saints and similar trifles. This the people rightly loathe, and so they walk out on them immediately after the reading of the gospel. A few of the better ones [preachers] have begun now to speak about good works, but they still say nothing about the righteousness of faith, about faith in Christ, and about the consolation of consciences . . . .On the contrary, in our [Lutheran] churches all the sermons deal with topics like these: repentance, fear of God, faith in Christ, the righteousness of faith, consolation of consciences through faith, the exercise of faith, prayer (what it should be like and that everyone may be completely certain that it is efficacious and is heard), the cross, respect for the magistrates and all civil orders, the distinction between the kingdom of Christ (the spiritual kingdom) and political affairs, marriage, the education and instruction of children, chastity, and all the works of love. From this description of the state of our churches it is possible to determine that we diligently maintain churchly discipline, godly ceremonies, and good ecclesiastical customs.[2]

What is interesting about Melanchthon's observations is that he concludes with an additional consequence of faithful proclamation, that it creates the unity and well-being of the church. Other written Lutheran sources also describe the value and centrality of the preacher/listener relationship. Two of the other settings where this relationship is affirmed in clear detail today are in the vocational vows of those who are ordained, and congregational affirmations of these vows in the ordination and installation services of the Evangelical Lutheran Church in America.

Although forms of these services have changed and evolved over the centuries, the same basic things are stated. There are repeated references to the gospel and preaching in the service. The preacher/listener relationship is observed in the ordination service with this affirmation of the presider to the people: "Let it be acclaimed that *(name here)* is ordained a minister in the Church of Christ. He/She has Christ's authority to preach the Word and administer the Sacraments, serving God's people." And the people affirm this by responding: "Amen. Thanks be to God."[3]

In the service of installation, visual means of describing the preacher's responsibilities are enacted in this way: "The presiding minister escorts the newly installed pastor. . . . They proceed to the pulpit, where a representative of the congregation says, "You have been called to be among us to proclaim the good news."[4]

One of the documents that describes and points to the reciprocal nature of the preacher/listener relationship is the "Model Constitution for Congregations of the Evangelical Lutheran Church."[5] All ELCA congregations have some form of this constitution, which makes a brief and pertinent study document for all members. The document ascertains that certain individuals are specifically called to preach, and the congregation is asked to confirm the message of that preaching in their corporate lives.

In the section of the congregation's constitution that is entitled "Statement of Purpose," "Word of God" language is repeatedly used in different ways. Specific references to preaching include "To participate in God's mission, this congregation as a part of the Church shall: Worship God in proclamation of the Word . . . ."[6] Further on in the same chapter: "To fulfill these purposes, this congregation shall: a. Provide services of worship at which the Word of God is preached and the sacraments administered."[7]

The responsibilities of the called pastor also begin this way: "Consistent with the faith and practice of the Evangelical Lutheran Church in America, a. Every ordained minister shall: 1) preach the Word . . . ."[8] The list of the ordained minister's basic duties concludes with one "shall" that may provide some interesting links to preaching, since it refers to the minister's public speech: "5) [every minister shall:] speak publicly to the world in solidarity with the poor and oppressed, calling for justice and proclaiming God's love for the world."[9]

In studying the relationship between preacher and listeners, the ordering of responsibilities in this congregation's constitution, chapter by chapter, clearly indicates that the primary choices and responsibilities for preaching in a congregation originate with the congregation's members. The preaching they hear is a response to their basic pastoral choices.

And who is listening?

The nature and state of the sermon *listener* receives little attention in historical Lutheran statements on preaching. Traditionally, the sermon listener is perceived as a silent recipient of God's Word. However, this pulpit perspective views the listener as basically passive and with no role in the preaching event other than acceptance of the proclamation. Luther expressed little patience for reluctant or absent listeners. Many of his sermons soundly berate the people for what he thought was their stubbornness in refusing God's Word.

Preachers often express frustration about having little insight into who their listeners are and what their spiritual needs and questions may be. Sermon feedback from listeners that might assist future sermon preparation is significantly limited. The most response many preachers ever hear is "Good sermon, pastor!" or "I really enjoyed that sermon!" or one of the more nerve-racking responses for the preacher: "Interesting sermon."

At one level the inscrutability of the listeners has partly to do with the mystery of preaching and the work of the Holy Spirit. It is impossible to control the interpretation of one's sermonic words to any great extent once they are "out there" among the people. Who knows what impact and changes the preached Word might create in the listeners? The listeners themselves can hardly comprehend this! The effect of one sermon or years of listening to sermons may have unexpected and uncharted effects in the listeners' lives, which are only rarely accessible to the preacher. The lack of feedback, however, is primarily fed by the reality that preaching is a monologue in which one speaks and others listen. Lutherans have not traditionally viewed their role with the preacher as involving consistent verbal feedback.

Only near the latter part of the 20th century did preaching in the Lutheran church even begin to challenge the passive role of the sermon listener. Preachers began to elicit listener responses in dialogue sermons. Some even began encouraging the brave few to respond verbally, using the preacher question/listener response pattern of preaching that is more common in African-American preaching traditions.

But the preacher seeking verbal involvement from listeners continues to be a rarity today. How then does one get at the sermon listener's participation in the preaching event?

One thing listeners bring to a sermon is their *expectations* of the sermon. If asked, listeners will offer a variety of responses. Here is a partial list of what parishioners come to hear, or at least hope to hear, in a sermon:

- inspiration
- what the Bible says
- being renewed or "filled up" for the rest of the week (the gas station metaphor of sermonic expectations)
- being "fed," a logical response to the Bread of Life among us
- instructions on what to do, how to live life
- how to make ethical decisions in daily life as a Christian
- challenge
- comfort
- explanation of difficult issues
- a call to the individual and the congregation to lead lives patterned on Jesus Christ
- conviction of sin
- calls to unite
- an address to family issues and relationships
- realistic discussion of sinful human nature[10]

These expectations vary from person to person but certainly provide the backdrop against which weekly preaching happens. Expectations are disappointed when the listeners hear preaching that they deem:

- too theologically abstract;
- overly focused on the preacher's personal experiences or theology;
- insufficiently based on the Bible;
- irrelevant because the questions of the people are not addressed;
- cowardly, if the preacher continually avoids working with the difficult biblical texts found in the lectionary;

- biased in terms of such things as gender, ethnicity, political views, experiences of life, and the congregation's realities;
- preached outside the limits of what the congregational generally thinks is a "Lutheran sermon," whether in style, tone, or theology;
- too intimate in nature or too disinterested;
- lacking in the personal, genuine witness to Jesus Christ on the part of the preacher.

Besides listener expectations, where else does the dissonance occur between preacher and listeners in the preaching event? A major level of conflict occurs when the preacher is either unwilling or unable to "exegete the congregation" in the interests of good proclamation. What does this mean? Just as the preacher will spend time studying and untangling the intricacies of a biblical text for a sermon, so also the preacher must carefully "read" the congregation's life in its corporate and individual meanings and activities.[11] By way of example, think of those family members and relatives attending a funeral at which the preacher extols the virtues of the deceased who, by any accounts, was much less than virtuous. The sermon that has read the congregation well will be able to reflect back accurately to the people their lives and the call to live in the gospel.

Bridging the gap

Given both the traditional and documented views of preaching in the Lutheran church, what are the options for lessening the homiletical differences between preachers and listeners found in so many places? That the question should be posed at all says something about the restlessness in the pews today concerning preaching and the preachers' own concerns about their sermonic ministry. So how can useful changes be made? Are there also reasons for *not* making changes in the acts of proclamation and listening?

First, over the last fifteen years increased attention has been devoted to the sermon listener. Who is listening? Why? Is it enough to listen and remain silent, or does the sermon listener also need a vantage point from which to speak and possess methods by which to do that? Writers on the theory and practices of preaching have produced some works that review preaching as a two-way conversation.

Preaching is now being linked with the way the listener may also respond and proclaim the gospel. Two writers in particular, John McClure and Lucy Atkins Rose[12] have written books on this topic. By looking at a more egalitarian, conversational frame for preaching, other topics also must be considered, such as pastoral and lay authority, training, and decisions on text choices and topics.

Second, if both preacher and listeners commit to changing the traditional format for preaching, how might this be done? There are several possibilities, all of which take time and planning and extend the solo work of the pastor's sermon preparation into the congregation. Some of these are:

- Teaching listening skills. Listening is not innate, nor is it a gift; it must be learned. There are a number of steps that everyone can learn in this most crucial part of homiletical communication.[13]
- Do a basic congregational survey that reveals the general thinking about the role of the sermon and its function in the church. (See a sample survey at the end of this chapter.)
- Establish biblical text study groups that study lectionary texts one to three weeks ahead of the Sunday on which the texts will be preached. The group will include preacher and selected parishioners (chosen on a rotating basis) who will study the texts and consider how the texts intersect with the congregation's life and ministry.
- Invite selected groups to debrief the sermon with the preacher after it has been delivered.
- Use the lectionary texts assigned for the upcoming Sunday's preaching and read portions of them in the week to come at all meetings and functions of the parish. The texts can be used as

devotional material, material for discernment on difficult issues, and as themes for various gatherings.

• Use sermon feedback forms.[14]

Will these things bridge the gaps between preacher and listeners? In some ways, they are certainly a step towards ensuring a more realistic form of proclamation. Doing some of these feedback gatherings is also a way of affirming both the congregation and pastor's constitutional and corporate views of who they are as a household of faith. It should be noted, however, that preaching has *always* been the one unpredictable element in congregational life. God's Spirit will blow where it wishes, as John's Gospel notes, and who knows in what ways this affects preaching?

Discarding and retaining

New challenges for preaching invite us to assess what is useful and what is not in proclaiming the faith that redeems us. The era of the "great models of name preachers" is gone, and listeners are called to relocate their responsibilities in preaching. This means attention to context, to our faith community as it gathers itself and as it sends its members into their varied worlds. It means looking at what our ecumenical neighbors are doing in preaching and seeing if there are possibilities and new directions that might influence and inform our own proclamation.

It also means asking what is essential and must be preserved in our proclamation. One possibility that always exists for the preacher, however uncomfortable for all concerned, is that preaching may entail a radical challenge that sets the preacher *against* the congregation. This has sometimes been described as "prophetic preaching," although perhaps a better term might be found, since all good preaching is prophetic by nature. Still, there are times when the gospel's validity and truth are injured in a faith community, and proclamation is called to address that fact in a prophetic way.

Likewise, the congregation's ears must always be attuned to inappropriate or false expressions of the gospel from the pulpit. So great is this responsibility that the congregation's constitution sees false statements about the gospel as reason for removing a pastor "on grounds of doctrine."[15] This is why an appropriate measure of theological training is always essential for both the ordained and the layperson so that the gospel may be preached faithfully.

The challenge of preaching today is to move beyond traditional models to preaching that is given birth and carried within community context and faithful to the lives of the listeners. It means, finally, that the preaching will enable the listener's lives to "preach" by way of confessing and living out their faith in the radically pluralistic world in which they live. If preaching stops at the door as the faithful leave, they leave only as "sponge Christians," capable of receiving, but giving nothing of themselves and their faith.

The X factor

Preaching, for all its domesticity and familiarity, can still surprise us. Listeners and preachers are often startled at how the proclamation of Jesus Christ publicly among them affects their lives and relationships. In some cases, people might find themselves radically challenged or graciously comforted even by a sermon that has, for the most part, been ill-prepared or missed its mark. In other cases, a powerfully preached sermon has the ability to change everything for one listener, while another may view the sermon as nonessential. Such is the mystery of the interaction between preacher and listener.

Lutherans have not reflected deeply enough on the role of the Holy Spirit and the Spirit's inspiration in preaching. Luther's affirmation of preaching as the primary means of grace, the central means of knowing God, has been eclipsed to some extent. Listeners may miss the fact that both a well-prepared sermon and a fiery and unprepared one are capable of hosting the Spirit's work among us. Today it is this reappraisal of the Spirit's power that is most capable of affecting our views of preaching and the relationship of preacher and listener. It is this presence of the Spirit that invites the preacher and listener to speak and hear in more thoughtful and heartfelt ways. It is this Spirit that invites us to life-giving surprise through the preaching event!

For personal reflection

1. What do you appreciate about the biblical and historically Lutheran understandings of preaching? What is a problem for you?
2. As a preacher, what do you find most difficult about the sermon preparation task?
3. If you are a sermon listener, how do your expectations of a sermon match with the list provided earlier in this chapter?
4. In looking at Melanchthon's list of Lutheran sermon topics, what surprises you? How many of these do you hear preached today?
5. If you and others were to study your church's constitution and the services of ordination and installation, what questions would you raise about the actual practices of preaching in your setting as compared to the wording of these documents concerning preaching?
6. What do you think of the direction towards "sermon as conversation"?
7. How do you understand the role of the Holy Spirit in preaching? (Reading the Third Article of the Creed as well as Luther's discussions of the Holy Spirit in his Large and Small Catechisms will provide helpful background for this discussion.)

For further reflection in your congregation

See the survey that was developed for a local Lutheran congregation on page 85. The results were used to discuss sermon expectations and preparation and the congregation's proclamation ministry.

6

"Only Jesus": The Elusive and Intimate God

". . . she turned around and saw Jesus standing there, but she did not know that it was Jesus."

◁≫ *John 20: 14b*

One of the most striking themes permeating the New Testament documents is the repeated inability of human beings to recognize Jesus' reality before and after his resurrection, even when he was with them physically. Friend and foe are continually asking him to prove his identity. Many experienced a disjuncture between what they knew him to be—Mary's son, Rabbi—and who he claimed to be through his words and actions. Mary Magdalene does not recognize him in the garden following his resurrection. Why? Perhaps her eyes were too blurred with tears to see. She seems not to have even recognized his voice. How could she expect to see him alive and standing before her in that place? It is not surprising that she experiences a kind of tunnel vision, the kind of failure to recognize someone who suddenly appears before us in an unaccustomed setting.

The disciples on the road to Emmaus likewise do not recognize Jesus until they look in retrospect at what he said and did in their presence. Some deliberately choose not to recognize Jesus. When Peter is confronted about his relationship with Jesus, he says vehemently: "Woman, I do not know him" (Luke 22:57). Saul's furious persecution of Jesus' followers also results in a confrontation on the Damascene road where he fearfully asks, "Who are you, Lord?" (Acts 9:5). The disciples who witnessed the event of the Transfiguration are also caught between the glory of the moment and the aftermath, when quite simply the Gospel writer says,

"Suddenly when they looked around, they saw no one with them anymore, but only Jesus" (Mark 9:8).

There are, however, two other groups who *do* recognize Jesus. The New Testament names a number of outcasts: the desperate, the forsaken and marginalized who immediately perceive him for what and who he is. Sometimes these people went to great lengths to be close to him and respond to him. Zacchaeus climbed a tree; a woman with perfume in her hands sneaked into a dinner party where he sat; the political ruler of one region cared less about his rank and more for his sick child's sake as he acknowledged Jesus' power. Such people often recognized and confessed his name and divinity before the disciples had a clue about what was going on! And the biblical writers assert that the demons recognize Jesus as well.

Preaching the question

Jesus himself challenged onlookers, curiosity seekers, the alienated and believers with his question, "Who do you say that I am?" One can look at Jesus' question and consider where the emphasis might fall, for it is a question rich in many meanings and possible answers.

- *WHO*—Is Jesus a human being? divine? both? of God or not?
- *YOU*—This emphasis draws the questioner into a place of responsibility and response. Can you or I affirm this Jesus as the Christ, the Son of God? as merely a "good person"? a prophet? a lunatic?
- *SAY*—What claims might people make of Jesus, both then and now? What understanding and experience of Christ do we reveal with our words?

What then, is at stake with Jesus' question when it comes to twenty-first century preaching? In all cases, whatever the responses, Jesus' question requires of us not simply knowledge of his identity but confession of it. The faith we proclaim in our communities is not simply a matter of intellectual assent or dissent. It is ultimately confessional in nature and understands "truth" as relationship with the person of Jesus Christ. This requires of us commitment and the willingness to live and speak of this relationship in all areas of our lives.

Why is this important now? We live in a world where faith claims abound and where those claims can be heard and seen on a moment to moment basis. Satellite-driven broadcasting and Internet access feed us news and views at an unprecedented volume and speed. In the midst of this global reality, we are challenged to consider our own faith claims and their implications for all expressions of life, be they religious, political, personal or communal. Isolation from interdenominational and intrafaith conversations is impossible if one is open to the work of the Spirit in the world. The Lutheran preacher and listener, more than ever, must ask how we understand Jesus' question, for it is the foundation to our responses in this global faith conversation. How will we bring the person and the reality of Jesus the Christ, child of God, into dialogue with the world and with our own personal context?

A theology of the cross

From a Lutheran belief and proclamation perspective, one rich and meaningful response to Jesus' question that we can bring to these religious and cultural conversations is our proclamation of "a theology of the cross," rather than a "theology of glory." What does this mean? It means that what we say about God as Christians *always* begins and ends with the reality and mystery of the cross. Living, ministering, suffering, dying, and rising are the patterns of Jesus' life that provide the pattern of a true faith life to us who live in the post-Resurrection times. Any efforts to answer Jesus' question without the reality of the cross are without merit.

Those who preach the theological alternative, sometimes termed "a theology of glory," tend to focus only on God's triumphs and on our human ability to live a "victorious" Christian life. But this theology denies the reality of sin in our lives and places too much emphasis on our own ability to affect our own salvation. It discounts or downplays the effects of sin, suffering, and death. Lutheran theology is clear that without the cross there can be no "glory," and Christ's death is in vain.

Yet, while Lutherans proclaim the answer to Jesus' question always moves through the cross, the *ways* in which this proclamation happens are numerous. Because this is so, the best preaching looks repeatedly at the many interpretive lenses that exist in any congregation's life and context. How best to respond to Jesus' question? What will these people and this preacher, in this time and place, find most helpful in grasping some sense of the immense reality of Jesus Christ? Are there useful theological works and challenges from outside a given church community that need to be heard by those believers?

One cross event, multiple voices

Available interpretations of the life and acts of Jesus Christ are multiple in the twenty-first century. Some come from communities and concerns that have developed theological resources and responses to Jesus' question out of their own lived experiences and the struggles of faith. Some theological perspectives have been developed out of cross-cultural, global, and pluralistic reassessments of the world. Others such as John Douglas Hall and David Tracey look particularly at the meanings of gospel and culture today. Other interpretations arise less specifically and more spontaneously from American popular culture.

In terms of the first type, Lutheran proclaimers and listeners now have access to a growing number of books and human resources that look at faith life from unique perspectives, such as feminist, womanist, African-American, Asian, liberation (sometimes associated with church life in South American faith communities), gay-lesbian-bisexual, and mujerista.[1] Their theological works offer challenge and new insights for Lutheran proclaimers for such topics as naming God, looking at the cross event in different ways, demanding new structures of community that will offer more realistic support, justice-making, and faith-living patterns of life.

Many Lutherans in ethnically and religiously homogenous churches are often unaware of these resources. Studied and wisely used they can definitely challenge Lutheran preachers and listeners to grow and change as the Spirit guides. For example, many Lutherans may be unfamiliar with the "womanist" perspective, which refers to the theological concerns and writings of African-American female theologians[2] and "mujerista," which refers to the theology done by South American female theologians. Theological resources written by African-American male theologians, such as James Cone and Dwight Hopkins, offer insights that are necessary to the conversation and life of believers. Their writings pose significant challenges to listeners regarding society, justice, views of God, and community.

An example of one theological perspective emerging from some of the writings of several different African-American representatives relates to the theme of the role of suffering. Suffering is a commonly accepted aspect of Christian faith, which looks to the sufferings of Jesus on the cross as a model for our own faith life. However, these theologians ask: Is it necessary to value suffering? Is suffering, in and of itself, redemptive in any way? Can we accept Jesus' death on the cross apart from endorsing suffering as the primary focus of the cross event? The key question from these communities becomes this: If we validate suffering as a theologically "positive" thing, are we then running the risk of validating our own ethnic and gender suffering by accepting a lesser role as people of faith in human terms? Such questions lead us to wonder what other meanings of Jesus' death might be forgotten or unexplored.

Feminist theologians ask a related question with regard to redemption: If the silent suffering of Jesus on the cross is always validated as the sole model for what redemption means, what does it say to women who are the majority of the victims of domestic violence? Should that traditional view of the cross be accepted, and should women, as a consequence, continue to subject themselves to this model of violence and silence? Or, is there another way to think about the cross that is life-giving, healing, and nonabusive?

One Bible, many views

Responding to Jesus' question homiletically means seeking and reflecting his identity to a faith community, and it means asking how the Bible is being preached. Different types of faith communities, whether Lutheran or other branches of the ecumenical tree, tend to have "favorite" Bible texts, that play a role in what is and is not preached.

Preachers and listeners alike may want to think of periodically choosing biblical texts outside the assigned lectionary texts as a way of exploring these themes. Thematic or "series" preaching can be a way to focus attention on a topic or issue of interest. A series can also focus on a particular biblical theme or on one particular book. Those who do such series preaching often report a rise in listener interest, as listeners look forward to the "next" part or installment in the series.

Without living representatives of different theological perspectives available in a community, the Bible provides the key means of opening the conversation about these views. A 20th book on the lectionary, written from a liberation theology perspective,[3] clearly points out that it is easy to form the views of a community by what readings from the Bible are omitted, as well as what is included. A student/pastor from the African Methodist Episcopal tradition startled his Lutheran classmates recently by describing an evangelist in AME tradition who had made a commitment to herself to learn to preach on every book in the Bible! How would such a venture change and reform one's own theology and preaching? How would this venture make it easier to learn the theological views of other communities?

What culture has to say about a popular Jesus

One of the more fascinating tributaries of theology that flows into the lives of Lutheran listeners and preachers is what the surrounding culture says about who Jesus is and what he can do. These cultural artifacts and assertions about Jesus are sometimes amusing, sometimes useful, and sometimes run counter to what Lutherans understand Jesus to be and do. What are some of these cultural pictures of Jesus, and what do they have in common?

Over the past several years, the initials "WWJD" (What Would Jesus Do?) have emerged on signs, bracelets, and bumper stickers. Based on this question, Jesus is used as an ethical guide to life choices. The question itself first found popular expression in the early 20th Century book, *In His Steps*, by Charles M. Sheldon. This novel describes the moral crisis created in a church one Sunday morning when a homeless man who asks for recognition and acceptance confronts the pastor and people. The hidden assumption in this phrase is that human beings will make the right choices based on their reading of Jesus.

Another favorite is the poem "Footprints in the Sand." Here God/Jesus is pictured as a type of anonymous Savior in desperate and lonely human situations. The poem has been sold on bathmats, jewelry, cards, printed on flags, and read at countless funerals. (It has also been put on the banned list of permissible poetry in Gettysburg Lutheran Seminary preaching classes!) Some of the poem's spin-offs on the Internet range from the humorous to the outrageous. The poem describes someone experiencing grief and loss walking on the seashore. According to the poem, the single visible set of footprints are God's footprints, and the person who is experiencing difficulty is being "carried" through their grief. The theology in this poem focuses on a very individualistic understanding of faith that is difficult to preach with integrity. Where are the multiple sets of footprints that witness to the presence of God's communion of saints? Could the footprints be someone else's besides God's? Where are the challenges to the believer that God might be placing before the person in a time of loss? Where is the cross represented in this poem?

Periodically, a book from the "Christian" genre will reach the best-seller list. One such recent book is *The Prayer of Jabez*. Based on 1 Chronicles 4:10, the prayer is a bold request for God's blessing. Using examples from his own life and ministry, the author implies that praying such a prayer will always lead to receiving what we ask for in faith. The theology in the book seems to displace any "theology of the cross" by drawing a cause-and-effect line between the believer's requests and receiving what is requested, sometimes known as "prosperity theology." It is a theology that cannot adequately address the human experiences of loss, deprivation, and the inscrutability of God.

What do these cultural views of Jesus say? Certainly they say he continues to be a topic of conversation. Perhaps more unsettling, however, is that these books, slogans, and poems also give human beings the impression they can easily know the mind of God and also manipulate the actions of God. There is a kind of specificity and reduced view of God in many of these popular versions of Jesus that runs counter to the elusive figure that one finds in the New Testament.

The certitude about Jesus that popular cultural views express is not the Jesus preached in Lutheran pulpits, the Jesus who might very well offer a question instead of an answer and who dwells in the deserted and poverty-stricken places as well as the lush and rich ones.

For reflection

1. Why do you think Jesus' identity is such a topic of discussion and dispute in the New Testament?
2. How have you heard the "theology of the cross" preached? Have you heard a "theology of glory" preached? Where?
3. Of the different theological voices from a number of faith communities described in the chapter, which of these are

familiar to you? unfamiliar? Have you heard any of these views expressed in preaching?

4. Which portions of the Bible have you never heard preached? Which would you like more preaching on? Why?

5. Can you think of other popular cultural reflections or expressions of Jesus besides those listed in this chapter? What do you like or dislike about them? How do they compare to the person of Jesus you hear preached on Sunday?

6. Would you be interested in preaching or listening to a sermon series? Why or why not? What "series" topics might interest you?

7. How might the lectionary provide the basis for a sermon series?

7

Lutheran Voices:
Witnesses to Life

"For I decided to know nothing among you except Jesus Christ, and him crucified."

➤ *1 Corinthians 2:2*

"Who do you say that I am?" asks Jesus. The question is one that needs to be perpetually addressed to our preaching and listening. It is a question that calls both proclaimer and listener to account. The question echoes down the centuries and still sounds in our ears amidst multiple religious, cultural, personal truth claims. In some ways, our postmodern world is little different from the world of St. Paul, with its competing religious claims and multiple calls to faith. Paul acknowledged those as he stood among the Athenians and noted their many gods, including the altar "to an unknown god." In that setting Paul told them "the good news about Jesus and the resurrection" (see Acts 17).

Jesus' question provokes some anxiety in us, for it is a "standing" question and the vast possibilities it presents for preaching and listening are overwhelming. His question engages us in struggling with the answers and the tensions it involves. Luther readily admitted his own reservations about the enormity of preaching the gospel, saying, "I would rather be stretched upon a wheel or carry stones than preach one sermon. For anyone who is in this office will always be plagued; and there I have often said that the damned devil and not a good man should be a preacher. But we are stuck now."[1]

Nevertheless, Jesus' question leads both preacher and listeners on to the possibilities of ever-deepening and widening views of God and life. It is an open-ended process of new insights, growth, and relationship with God. It is a discernment process that can inevitably lead to frustration, misunderstanding, and more questions. Yet, that is to be expected. One astute theologian offers comfort for this task:

> Our natural theologies are always wrong. . . .Yet, it is right to build them. Each of them constitutes a step on the way to brighter illumination, and they are necessary steps. . . .Our real dangers lie in failing to embrace our successive revelations. As Charles Williams once wrote, "Unless devotion is given to a thing which must prove false in the end, the thing that is true in the end cannot enter."[2]

Jesus' question is a call to understand our faith priorities, preach them, confess them, and live them. These are things *both* preacher and listener are called to do. The question perpetually demands that we check how human community, circumstances, and context affect our responses to Jesus' query. Luther noted this dynamic, changeable aspect of preaching in response to its work of witnessing to Jesus Christ:

> "A preacher is like a carpenter. His tool is the Word of God. Because the materials on which he works vary, he ought not always pursue the same course when he preaches. For the sake of the variety of his audience he should sometimes console, sometimes frighten, sometimes scold, sometimes soothe, etc."[3]

Lutherans look at their own preaching heritage and see it for the challenging gift that it is, the gift that invites us to God's salvation and a new way of life. Luther described the power of change inherent in God's Word with this lyrical description:

> For the Word of God is the true holy object. Indeed, it is the only one we Christians know and have. . . .But God's Word is the treasure that makes everything holy. By it all saints have themselves been made holy. At whatever time God's Word is taught, preached, heard, read, or pondered, there the person, the day, and the work is hallowed, not

on account of the external work but on account of the Word that makes us all saints.[4]

Valuing the heritage

What are the features of this heritage of proclamation we have received, this unique Lutheran homiletical perspective we share with the world? One of the most "recent" definitions of a Lutheran sermon is found in *Manual on the Liturgy*, which defines worship practices based on *Lutheran Book of Worship*. The statement reads:

> The Sermon is the living voice of the Gospel today. As God's appointed speaker and the chief teacher of the congregation, the pastor sheds light on the meaning of the Scriptures and shows how their message applies to the contemporary situation.[5]

While any given Lutheran sermon may provide many variants of expression of our historical preaching heritage (see Chapter Three), Lutheran proclamation has generally included the following elements over the centuries:

- Valuing the Word of God in all its expressions, but particularly its chief expression which is the person of Jesus Christ.
- Understanding the biblical description of preaching that faith is created by hearing the gospel preached.
- Delighting in the tensions and paradoxes that characterize the various aspects of humanity's relationship to God. These include: justification and sanctification; the condition of humanity as sinner-yet-saved; law and gospel; grace and faith.
- Viewing preaching as the center and radical change agent in public worship, and the preacher as a conduit of that process.
- Expressing a receptivity to the influences of human culture and life and therefore contextual in nature.
- Clarity about the reality of sin, death, and the powers of evil and names them as such.

- Proclamation by lay or ordained, female or male, that focuses on the single person (usually) witnessing and proclaiming the gospel from the pulpit.
- The means through which God calls, redeems, establishes, and changes individual believers and the church at large.

Lutheran preaching today: Where to?

We know the possibilities and beauties of our preaching heritage, but do today's sermon listeners actually view preaching in the same way as their Reformation forebears? What is the level of awareness among Lutherans about the meaning, value, and formative powers of preaching? What have today's listeners and preachers added to the understanding of preaching's possibilities, and what have they dismissed as nonessential or problematic? These emerging changes and pressure points found in 21st-century preaching may be summarized as follows:

- The recognition that all preaching relates to Jesus' core question of "Who do you say that I am?" This means the preacher and the listener are called to respond confessionally to the world at large, not just within a given faith community or Christian tradition. *Confessional* preaching, listening, and living invite believers to live out the gospel in the postmodern context.
- The recognition of more diverse cultural and ecumenical forms of preaching, fostered in part by new worship resources and more eclectic congregational membership.
- Borrowing from the vocabularies of science, medicine, psychology, and sociology to describe life dynamics and faith. For example, the reality of "sin" takes into consideration terms such as "alienation," "separation," and "illness."
- Unease among listeners who question the authority of the preacher. Minority communities, in particular, have called the church to address the issue of authority and privilege when represented by the pulpit.

- The use of inclusive language that is more sensitive to the varied representations of life-style, gender, and circumstances of the listeners. In part, this has been prompted by more inclusive language in biblical translations and liturgical materials.[6] Primarily, it is an attempt to be faithful to the gospel principle of the inclusion of all people.
- Paying attention to the metaphors, biblical or otherwise, which are used in preaching to define the church, such as "family." Metaphors, which depend on cultural interpretations and symbols, can make of faith communities something less than the church and are not inclusionary in a gospel sense.
- Using a Bible that is filtered through the lectionary, multiple translation options, and attention to biblical preaching options outside the lectionary as well.
- Different media usages that include technology in various forms, which can decenter or diffuse the usual focus on the person preaching.
- Experiencing the pressures to create proclamation form and contents that are responsive to the identified needs of evangelism. This includes preaching that addresses Christian "seekers," in addition to those who are lifelong believers.
- The use of different sermon forms in different combinations, including dialogue sermons, dramas/skits, interviews with guests such as missionaries, children's sermons, the use of computer-generated programs, and big screen images. These efforts acknowledge the listeners' active participation in proclamation.
- The disappearance of the pulpit in some churches, replaced by a preacher walking around among listeners, sitting down and talking, or using the altar as a preaching place. This is a response to the growing sense of the need for intimacy and vulnerability when proclaiming the gospel.
- Responds more to the ethical and moral question of listeners: "How to live the holy life?"

Lutheran proclamation faces many challenges at the beginning of this new century. It is an area of Christian life and practice that is receiving careful scrutiny by many homiletical writers.[7] It is also something that is becoming recognized more realistically as the responsibility of *both* preacher and listener. David Lose, a Lutheran preacher and teacher, concludes that "preaching that seeks to be both faithful to the Christian tradition and responsive to our pluralistic postmodern context is best understood as the public practice of confessing faith in Jesus Christ."[8]

Jesus asks: "Who do you say that I am?" And the question we then ask ourselves is this: "What do the preacher and people say to that?"

For reflection

1. For what reasons do you think Luther both preached *and* resisted the act of preaching?
2. In your context, how has the preaching event matched up with the preaching values inherited from the Reformation era?
3. Review the list on pp. 82-83. Do any of these statements characterize preaching in your faith community? If so, which ones? Which of these do you appreciate? Which do you have problems with? Why?
4. What metaphors are used in your church's preaching to describe your church—"Family"? "Community"? "Household of faith"? "Communion of saints"? "Priesthood of all believers"? What picture of the church does each of these terms give, and what are their strengths and weaknesses?
5. How do you think current trends in church organization have affected the sermon? the preaching event?
6. What do you think is meant by "confessional preaching"?
7. How have your views of Jesus' question been changed by this book?
8. How have your views of preaching changed, if at all?

Appendix:
Assessing the Sermon

Below are four different tools that congregations and pastors can use in discussing and analyzing the act of preaching, the use of the Bible, and specific sermons.

Tool 1—What is a Lutheran Sermon?

This survey was developed for a local Lutheran congregation. The results were used to discuss sermon expectations and preparation and the congregation's proclamation ministry.

1. What do you hope to hear in a "good" sermon?

2. What or whose points of view do you think a sermon should represent?

3. What do you think is the role of the Bible in preaching?

4. What function(s) should a sermon play in the life of a congregation? in your life?

Any additional thoughts you wish to add:

The tools on pages 85-89 can be modified and/or reproduced for local use.

Tool 2—Proclamation Evaluation Form

Date: Setting:

Preacher: Listener:

Part 1

1. What was the FOCUS of the sermon? (Main idea, thought, image etc.)

2. What was the FUNCTION of the sermon? (How did the preacher want it to work in the lives of the listeners?)

3. How did the preacher use the TEXT(S)?

4. What was the preacher doing THEOLOGICALLY?

5. Did the sermon reflect the LITURGICAL CONTEXT?

6. How did the preacher use LANGUAGE (biblically, personally, theologically, imaginatively)?

7. Was GOD the subject of the sermon? If so, how? If not, who or what was?

8. In order to improve this sermon, I would suggest:

9. Additional comments:

Part 2

Mark on each continuum your perception of the preacher and sermon. If something does not apply, write NA (Not Applicable).

I. The Preacher's Ethos

Believability   +-----------------------------------0
Self-disclosure   +-----------------------------------0
Appearance   +-----------------------------------0

II. Structure/Contents

Organization   +-----------------------------------0
Preached the text +-----------------------------------0
Clarity   +-----------------------------------0
Language use   +-----------------------------------0
Use of humor   +-----------------------------------0

III. Delivery

a) Paraverbal
Volume   +-----------------------------------0
Pitch   +-----------------------------------0
Pace   +-----------------------------------0
Enunciation   +-----------------------------------0
Inflection   +-----------------------------------0

b) Vocal Cues
Nonfluencies: Lack of +-----------------------------------0
(false starts, slips, etc.)
Filled Pauses: Lack of
(ah, umm)   +-----------------------------------0

c) Nonverbal
Eye Contact   +-----------------------------------0
Posture/Gestures   +-----------------------------------0
Body Language   +-----------------------------------0
Energy Level   +-----------------------------------0

Today as a listener, my mood is best characterized as: _____

_____

Tool 3—Categorize the Sermon

Choose one of the following categorical statements to rate the sermon. Consider what additional constructive comments you could offer.

Category One

Proclamation demonstrates outstanding preaching of the good news of God in Jesus Christ; inclusive language used with accuracy, insight, and superlative biblical basis. Demonstrates significant pastoral, missional, proclamatory, rhetorical and liturgical connections with listeners.

"This is one of the best sermons I have ever heard!"

Category Two

Proclamation demonstrates significant ability to proclaim the gospel message through the chosen biblical text. Language use is inclusive, accurate, and insightful. Connections with the listeners are demonstrated in good proclamatory, rhetorical, missional, pastoral and liturgical fashion.

"A satisfying Sunday sermon."

Category Three

Proclamation demonstrates only average ability to proclaim the good news. The listener may wonder where God is in this sermon. Biblical material shows only minimal connections with sermon. Preacher uses language in a manner that is minimally inclusive, accurate, and insightful, and shows only average or below average grasp of proclamatory context of listeners.

"This sermon isn't anything I'd remember beyond the narthex door."

Category Four

Proclamation contains only a few hints that the preacher has proclaimed the gospel. Preacher's words may not be heard as a sermon.

The biblical basis of the sermon is missing or misunderstood. And any contextual connections are generally missing. If I had a picture of this sermon it would remind me of a poster which shows a preacher in the pulpit . . . and Jesus sleeping in the front pew.[1]

"This person might do better in another area of ministry."

Category Five
Language and thinking demonstrate a clear "miss."
"We won't go there...."

Tool 4—Questions about the Bible for Preachers and Listeners[2]

1. What is the text trying to convince me/us of?

2. What does this passage assert about the human condition and about God?

3. How does this text seek to lay hold of me/us? That is, what literary and rhetorical devices does it employ in order to provoke me/us to faith? How does its structure and form make clear its confessional claims?

4. What do I/we know of the text's original setting and the history of its composition that helps to make sense of the claims it is making?

5. What do I/we feel actually happening to me/us as I/we read and study and pray about this passage? What is the text asking me/us to believe, to do, and to say?

6. And finally, do I/we believe what the text is saying and accept what it is asking, so that I/we can tell and ask it of others?

Notes

Introduction Who Do You Say That I Am?

1 *Fasciculus Morum:* A Fourteenth Century Preacher's Handbook, edited and translated by Siegfried Wenzel. (The Pennsylvania State University Press: University Park, 1989), Part I, Pride, page 41.

2 Significant authors from the twentieth and twenty-first centuries who look at society, culture and preaching issues include names such as H. Reinhold Niebuhr, Lucy Lind Hogan, Walter Kallestad, Tex Sample, Pierre Babin, Leonard Sweet, Lucy Rose, John McClure, David Buttrick, and David Lose.

3 For example, Dorothy Sayers, G. K. Chesterton, C. S. Lewis, Charles Williams, and Robert Farrar Capon

Chapter 1 The "Lutheran" in Lutheran Preaching

1 Gustaf Wingren, *The Living Word,* (Philadelphia: Fortress Press, 1960), p. 19.

2 James William Richard, *Philip Melanchthon* from *Heroes of the Reformation Series.* (New York: G. P. Putnam, The Knickerbocker Press, 1898).

3 *Book of Concord: The Confessions of the Evangelical Lutheran Church,* Edited by Robert Kolb and Timothy J. Wengert. (Minneapolis: Fortress Press, 2000). Hereafter noted as BC.

4 BC, Smalkald Articles, page 319.

5 See the pamphlet *The Use of the Means of Grace: A Statement on the Practice of Word and Sacrament,* (Minneapolis: ELCA, 1997).

6 Footnote 2, *Luther's Words,* Volume 52, Sermons II. Edited by Hans J. Hillerbrand and Helmut T. Lehmann. (Philadelphia: Fortress Press, 1974), p. ix. "The term postil came into usage in the early part of the sixteenth century. It was derived from the Latin *postilla,* "exposition," which in turn grew out of the standard phrase *post illa verba sacrae scripturae,* "according to these words of Sacred Scripture," with which the sermonic exposition customarily began.

7 "The Large [German] Catechism of Dr. Martin Luther," BC, p. 379

8 *Table Talk,* Volume 54, *Luther's Works.* Edited and translated by Theodore G. Tappert. General Editor Helmut T. Lehmann. (Philadelphia: Fortress Press, 1967).

9 *Luther's Works,* see especially Volumes 51 and 52

10 See *Sermons of Martin Luther,* edited by John Nicolas Lenker, Volumes I - VIII (Grand Rapids, Mich: Baker Book House, 1989).

11 See the polemic pamphlet entitled, "Infiltrating and Clandestine Preachers, 1532", in *Church and Ministry II,* Volume 40, LW. Edited by Conrad Bergendoff and General Editor Helmut T. Lehmann (Philadelphia: Muhlenberg Press, 1958), pp. 379 ff.

12 Martin Luther, *Sermons on the Gospel of St. John*, Chapters 1-4, Volume 22, LW, from the thirty-third sermon on the Gospel of John, September 14, 1538, pp. 400-401.

13 There are over 60 volumes in the premier collection of Luther's works, the *Weimar Ausgabe.*

14 It is significant to note that only a single entry related to the preacher is found in the main worship guide book accompanying *Lutheran Book of Worship.* The passage reads: "The Sermon is the living voice of the Gospel today. As God's appointed speaker and the chief teacher of the congregation, the pastor sheds light on the meaning of the Scriptures and shows how their message applies to the contemporary situation." *Manual on the Liturgy* (Minneapolis: Augsburg Publishing House, 1979), p. 221.

15 See the pioneering work of Carol Noren, *The Woman in the Pulpit* (Nashville: Abingdon, 1991).

16 The scriptural story of Jesus reading from the Book of Isaiah in his home synagogue reflects the lectionary practices of his day.

Chapter 2 It's the Gospel Truth

1 "Jesus Loves Me," Text by Anna Warner and music by William B. Bradbury. In *This Far By Faith: An African American Resource For Worship* (Minneapolis: Augsburg Fortress, 1999), Hymn # 249.

2 *Apology of the Augsburg Confession*, "Article XV: Human Traditions in the Church," BC, p. 229: 42.

3 BC, Smalkald Articles, page 319.

4 The word "canon" means an agreed-upon, authoritative collection of texts. It also points to the fact that the lectionary selections from the Bible are both "Bible" and literary choices made by committees over the centuries, e.g. two different sets of authorities.

5 *Revised Common Lectionary* prepared by the Consultation on Common Texts (Washington, D. C.: Abingdon Press, 1992). Hereafter, RCL.

6 For a rich and interesting history, see *Interpretation: A Journal of Bible and Theology*. Volume XXXI, April 1997, Number 12 for an issue-wide set of articles on the history and challenges of the lectionary.

7 See *Lutheran Book of Worship*, pp. 9-41 for a listing of all the Church Year texts according to the 1978 three-year lectionary cycle of texts. (Minneapolis: Augsburg Publishing House, Board of Publication, Lutheran Church in America, 1978). The 1978 cycle has been supplemented with congregational options to use the somewhat different text listings of the RCL.

8 For a useful discussion of the differences between lectionary and non-lectionary based preaching see David Buttrick, *A Captive Voice: The Liberation of Preaching* (Louisville: Westminster/John Knox Press, 1994) and Eugene L. Lowry,

Living with the Lectionary: Preaching Through the Revised Common Lectionary (Nashville: Abingdon Press, 1992).

Chapter 3 The Life of a Lutheran Sermon

1   Jacob Fry of Philadelphia Seminary wrote the first Lutheran English-language homiletics manual in 1893. It is a small booklet entitled *Rules and Notes in Homiletics. Printed for the Use of Students in the Evangelical Lutheran Theological Seminary,* Mt. Airy, PA. (Reading, PA: Henry N. Bieber, Printer, 1893). Among other things he urges the seminary preachers to mingle with cultivated English speakers so that they can learn to preach better in the American context!

2   This is a challenging question. L. Susan Bond in her work, *Trouble With Jesus: Women, Preaching and Christology* (St. Louis, MO: Chalice Press, 1999) makes the point that sermons may need to challenge bankrupt or self-serving forms of worship. In other words, preaching may have to assume a prophetic role that challenges the worship comfort zone and practices of those in attendance. There is ample evidence in the Old Testament that God became periodically fed up with great worship when it concealed faithlessness.

3   *Table Talk,* LW, Vol. 54, p. 138, No. 1322

4   Permission given by Pastor Fredrica Meitzen for use of this sermon.

Chapter 4 The Pulpit: A Look at the Preaching Furniture

1   Quote from John R. Throop, "Pulpits: A Place To Take Your Stand," from http://www.christianitytoday.com/yc/8y2/8y2048.html This is an excellent article on the history of pulpits and the varied materials from which they are made. The article includes a list of pulpit manufacturers. Also see the article by Kenton C Anderson, "The Place of the Pulpit," in *Preaching* 15:23-25, July-Aug, 1999.

2   Herman Melville, *Moby Dick,* (New York: Holt, Rinehart and Winston, 1964), Chapter, "The Pulpit," p. 39.

3   *Funk and Wagnalls Standard Dictionary, International Edition* (New York: Funk and Wagnalls Company, 1958), Volume II, p. 1021.

4   See the following resources for information on the history, design and theological functions of pulpits: Richard Carl Hoefler, *Designed for Worship* (Columbia, SC: The State Printing Company, 1963). Arthur Pierce Middleton, *New Wine in Old Skins: Liturgical Change and the Setting of Worship* (Wilton, CT: Morehouse-Barlow, 1988). Thomas M. Boyd, *Worship in Wood* (Chicago: Published by American Seating Company, MCMXXVII).

5   The plant is found in many different places throughout the world. It charmingly resembles a person in a pulpit. The Internet's various garden sites feature pictures and descriptions of it. The American painter Georgia O'Keefe painted some very striking pictures of this plant.

6   For example, see Martin Niemoller, *Dachau Sermons,* translated by Robert H. Pfeiffer (New York: Harper and Brothers, 1946).

7   Definition and information on this term were taken from the C-Span Internet site, specifically the C-Span Congressional Glossary. See http://www.c-span.org/guide/congress/glossary/bullypul.htm

Chapter 5 Who's Preaching? Who's Listening?

1   Martin Luther, *The Large Catechism* in BC 436: 38:1.

2   "Article XV: Human Traditions in the Church," *Apology of the Augsburg Confession,* BC 229:42-44.

3   "Ordination Service" in *Occasional Services* (Minneapolis: Association of Evangelical Lutheran Churches, 1982), p. 198.

4   Ibid, "Installation at Ordination," p. 199.

5   The most recent version of this is found on the ELCA web site: www.elca.org.

6   Ibid. Chapter 4, Statement of Purpose. C4.02.a.

7   Ibid., C4.03.a.

8   Ibid., See Chapter 9. The Pastor, C 9.03.a.

9   Ibid.

10   Thanks to some members of St. James Lutheran Church, Gettysburg, Pennsylvania, for their responses to the questions "What function(s) should a sermon play in the life of a congregation? in your life? This is from a Spring 2003 survey, the complete set of questions of which is found at the end of this chapter.

11   One of the best books that describes what is involved in this process for preacher and listener is by Leonora Tubbs Tisdale, *Preaching as Folk Art and Local Theology* (Minneapolis: Fortress Press, 1997).

12   See John McClure, *The Roundtable Church: Where Leadership and Preaching Meet.* (Nashville: Abingdon, 1995) and Lucy Rose, *Sharing the Word: Preaching in the Roundtable Church.* (Louisville: Westminster/John Knox, 1997).

13   There is a massive amount of work done in the field of listening by different types of researchers and scholars. The "bible" on listening was pioneered by Andrew Wolvin and Carolyn Gwynn Coakley, *Listening* (New York: Brown & Benchmark) Fifth Edition, 1996. See also this author's specifically theological work on listening called *Listening Ministry: Rethinking Pastoral Leadership* (Minneapolis: Fortress Press, 2001). These works focus not on listening and speaking, but specifically on the act of listening. Those seeking more information may also visit the Internet site of the International Listening Association at www. ILA.org.

14   See the assessment tools in "Appendix: Assessing the Sermon," pp. 85-89. These can be used as is or adapted for congregational use.

15   ELCA's "Model Constitution for the Congregation," Chapter 9, C9.05.5

Chapter 6 "Only Jesus": The Elusive and Intimate God

1   See L. Susan Bond, *Trouble With Jesus,* particularly Chapter Five, which analyzes these different areas of theology for their contributions to preaching.

2   See Jacqueline Grant, *White Women's Christ, Black Women's Jesus* (Atlanta: Scholars Press, 1989) and Kelly Douglas, *The Black Christ* (New York: Orbis Books, 1994). Alice Walker's novel *The Color Purple* also says a great deal theologically about African-American female theological perspectives.

3   Justo L. Gonzalez and Catherine Gunsalus Gonzalez, *Liberation and Preaching: The Pulpit and the Oppressed.* (Nashville: Abingdon Press, 1980).

Chapter 7 Lutheran Voices: Witnesses to Life

1   Martin Luther, "Sermon on the Twelfth Sunday of Trinity, 1531," LW, Volume 51, p. 222.

2   Mary McDermott Schideler, *Consciousness of Battle: An Interim Report on a Theological Journey.* (Grand Rapids, MI: William B. Eerdmans Publishing Company, 1970), p. 83.

3   Martin Luther, "Table Talk," LW, p. 31.

4   Martin Luther, "Ten Commandments," BC, p. 399.

5   Philip H. Pfatteicher, Carlos Messerli, *Manual on the Liturgy* (Minneapolis: Augsburg Publishing House, 1979), p. 221.

6   See the ELCA document *Principles for Worship* (Minneapolis: Augsburg Fortress Press, 2001). This work contains excellent materials on the use of language in worship and preaching.

7   See Thomas G. Long and Edward Farley, editors. *Preaching As a Theological Task: World, Gospel, Scripture. In Honor of David Buttrick.* (Louisville, KY: Westminster/John Know, 1996): Edited by Richard L. Eslinger, *Intersections: Post-Critcal Studies in Preaching* (Grand Rapids, MI: William B. Eerdmanns, 1994); *Theology for Preaching: Authority, Truth and Knowledge of God in a Postmodern Ethos,* (Nashville: Abingdon, 1997); David Lose, *Preaching Christ in a Postmodern Age* (William B. Eerdmanns, 2003).

8   David, Lose, *Confessing Jesus Christ: Preaching in a Postmodern World*, Ph. D. thesis, Princeton, NJ: Princeton Theological Seminary, 2000, p. 3.

Appendix: Assessing the Sermon

1   The author saw this poster on the office wall of Bishop Elmo Agrimson, Southeast Minnesota District of the American Lutheran Church Offices, St. Paul, Minnesota in the late 1970s.

2   I am indebted to Rev Dr. David Lose, homiletics teacher at Luther Seminary in St. Paul, Minnesota, for these questions. They are found in his doctoral thesis quoted earlier, pp. 196-197. He notes that his dual use of singular and plural pronouns is to emphasize that our views of the Bible are not ours alone but shared in community.

Bibliography

In addition to the multiple resources listed in the footnotes, the author also suggests the following resources.

Books

Allen, Ronald J. *Interpreting the Gospel: an Introduction to Preaching.* St. Louis, MO: Chalice Press, 1998

Brock, Rita Nakashima and Parker, Rebecca Ann. *Proverbs of Ashes: Violence, Redemptive Suffering, and the Search For What Saves Us.* Boston: Beacon Press, 2001

Craddock, Fred B. *Preaching.* Nashville: Abingdon Press, 1985.

Honeycutt, Frank G. *Preaching to Skeptics and Seekers.* Nashville: Abingdon Press, 2001

Long, Thomas G. *The Witness of Preaching.* Louisville: Westminster/John Knox Press, 1989

Taylor, Barbara Brown. *The Preaching Life.* Boston: Cowley Publications, 1993

Willimon, William H. and Hauerwas, Stanley. *Preaching to Strangers.* Louisville: Westminster/John Knox Press, 1992.

New Proclamation Series (Augsburg Fortress) Each year this series presents several different writers on a given season of the Church Year. The texts are based on *The Revised Common Lectionary (RCL)*

Sundays and Seasons (Augsburg Fortress) This is a text prepared for preachers and worship planners both. Both Sundays and festivals are listed and include history of the day, texts, suggested music, and a discussion of the themes of the texts and day.

Journals

Lectionary Homiletics This journal presents texts based on The *Revised Common Lectionary (RCL)* and does so from several perspectives, including exegetical studies, sermons on the same text from other preachers, literary quotes related to the texts, and illustrations for the texts.

Internet

Those surfing the Internet need only type in the following: "Preaching," "Sermons," or "Proclamation." There are literally thousands of sites to choose from. One example: *www.ltsg.edu.* This is the site for Lutheran Theological Seminary at Gettysburg. It keeps on file all sermons preached in the seminary's chapel and a faculty member, Dr. Richard P. Carlson, also provides biblical studies material related to the current year's texts.